Financial Planning Fundamentals: Analysis and Strategy for Success

Strategies for Achieving Financial Goals

Grace White

© Copyright 2024 - All rights reserved.

The content contained within this book may not be reproduced, duplicated or transmitted without direct written permission from the author or the publisher.

Under no circumstances will any blame or legal responsibility be held against the publisher, or author, for any damages, reparation, or monetary loss due to the information contained within this book, either directly or indirectly.

Legal Notice:

This book is copyright protected. It is only for personal use. You cannot amend, distribute, sell, use, quote or paraphrase any part, or the content within this book, without the consent of the author or publisher.

Disclaimer Notice:

Please note the information contained within this document is for educational and entertainment purposes only. All effort has been executed to present accurate, up to date, reliable, complete information. No warranties of any kind are declared or implied. Readers acknowledge that the author is not engaging in the rendering of legal, financial, medical or professional advice. The content within this book has been derived from various sources. Please consult a licensed professional before attempting any techniques outlined in this book.

By reading this document, the reader agrees that under no circumstances is the author responsible for any losses, direct or indirect, that are incurred as a result of the use of information contained within this document, including, but not limited to, errors, omissions, or inaccuracies.

Table of Contents

INTRODUCTION 5

CHAPTER I. Understanding Financial Planning Basics 6

    What is Financial Planning? 6

    Key Components of Financial Planning 12

    The Financial Planning Process 19

CHAPTER II. Setting Financial Goals 27

    Identifying Your Financial Goals 27

    Prioritizing and Balancing Goals 34

    SMART Financial Goals 41

CHAPTER III. Building a Budget 49

    Basics of Budgeting 49

    Creating a Sustainable Budget 56

    Adjusting the Budget for Changing Needs 62

CHAPTER IV. Saving and Investing 70

    The Role of Saving in Financial Planning 70

    Investment Fundamentals 76

    Diversifying Investments for Stability 83

CHAPTER V. Debt Management 92

    Types of Debt and Their Impact 92

    Strategies for Reducing Debt 98

    Maintaining a Healthy Credit Score 105

CHAPTER VI. Planning for Retirement 113

The Importance of Retirement Planning 113
Key Retirement Savings Options 119
Estimating Retirement Needs 124
CONCLUSION 131

INTRODUCTION

Financial planning is not merely a luxury in the fast-paced world of today; it is essential to attaining stability and reaching individual objectives. In order to empower readers to take control of their financial destiny, "Financial Planning Fundamentals: Analysis and Strategy for Success: Strategies for Achieving Financial Goals" offers a thorough manual for understanding key financial planning ideas. This book offers a methodical approach for anybody wishing to improve their financial well-being, from comprehending the fundamentals of budgeting and debt management to establishing specific financial objectives and making wise investment decisions.

This book provides a clear explanation of every component of financial planning, making it understandable to novices while yet offering insightful information to anyone with a basic understanding of personal finance. It walks readers through the crucial processes of developing and upholding a solid financial plan by emphasizing doable tactics, including retirement planning, reasonable and achievable financial goal-setting, and sustainable budgeting.

Additionally, readers will learn how to lower debt, safeguard their assets, and make wise investment and savings choices. This book is a useful resource for overcoming economic challenges and creating a route to success in a time when personal freedom and quality of life are strongly correlated with financial security. Let this guide serve as the starting point for achieving strategic goals and achieving financial empowerment.

CHAPTER I

Understanding Financial Planning Basics

What is Financial Planning?

The process of financial planning entails prudent money management in order to accomplish short- and long-term goals related to one's family, career, and personal life. In order to guarantee that people and families can preserve financial stability, follow their goals, and safeguard themselves against unanticipated events, it is a crucial discipline that integrates different facets of income, expenditure, saving, investing, and risk management. Fundamentally, financial planning consists of establishing financial objectives, assessing present financial circumstances, creating plans to close gaps between existing and desired financial states, and taking proactive measures to achieve these goals. People can not only survive financially but also flourish in a way that is consistent with their priorities and values thanks to this methodical approach to money management.

A thorough examination of a person's or household's existing financial situation is the first step in the financial planning process. Examining revenue sources, expenses, assets, liabilities, and net worth in detail is part of this evaluation. Since income and spending give a glimpse of cash flow, which is crucial for determining one's capacity to pay expenses and save, they are frequently the first areas of attention. Net worth, or the difference between one's possessions and debts, can be clearly seen by doing a detailed inventory of one's assets (real estate, investments, and savings accounts) and liabilities (debts, loans, and mortgages). The basis for identifying financial needs and establishing reasonable, reachable financial objectives is this study.

Setting goals gives financial planning direction and purpose, which makes it an essential step. Individuals' financial objectives might differ greatly depending on their age, way of life, family circumstances, and personal beliefs. These objectives could be saving for a child's education, purchasing a home, or having a comfortable retirement for some people. Others could place more importance on investing in a business, paying off debt, or setting up an emergency fund. Effective goals should be SMART—specific, measurable, achievable, relevant, and time-bound—regardless of the details. People may focus on what is really important to them financially and create a plan for reaching those goals when they have well-defined, unambiguous objectives. Furthermore, objectives may be short-, medium-, or long-term, and each type calls for a distinct plan of action. Long-term objectives are frequently focused on retirement or leaving a financial legacy, whereas short-term objectives could include saving for a trip or buying a house.

Setting goals makes budgeting a crucial part of the financial planning process. A budget is a thorough plan that specifies anticipated income and allows it to have different assets, savings, and expenses. It acts as a financial blueprint, assisting people in keeping spending under control, avoiding needless debt, and making sure that money is being spent in a way that supports their objectives. A deep comprehension of both fixed and variable expenses is necessary for effective budgeting. While variable expenses, like eating out or entertainment, can change from month to month, fixed expenses, like rent or mortgage payments, are prices that never change. People can find areas where changes may be required to align spending with financial priorities by keeping track of these expenses and comparing them to income. Intentional saving is another benefit of budgeting, which enables money to be set aside for investments, emergency cash, or other financially focused endeavors.

Another essential component of financial planning is saving, which forms the cornerstone of stability and financial security. Savings reduce dependency on credit and avert financial setbacks by acting as a buffer to meet unforeseen costs. An essential part of saving is having an emergency fund, which serves as a safety net in case of illness, unemployment, or other unanticipated events. Three to six months' worth of living expenses should ideally be covered by an emergency fund, while the precise amount may differ based on financial commitments and individual risk tolerance. People can save for specific objectives, like a down payment on a home, a child's education, or a future trip, in addition to emergency funds. Establishing distinct savings accounts for various purposes can assist people in avoiding taking money out of accounts intended for long-term objectives when urgent requirements emerge.

An equally important part of financial planning is investing, which uses a variety of financial instruments to increase wealth over time. Investments entail putting money into assets like stocks, bonds, real estate, or mutual funds with the hope of earning returns, as opposed to savings, which are normally held in low-risk, easily accessible accounts. Compared to conventional savings accounts, investments have the potential for larger returns, but they also come with a certain amount of risk. A key component of building wealth through investing is the compounding principle, which states that interest is earned on both the initial investment and accrued interest. People can use compounding to increase their wealth tremendously by beginning early and making regular investments over time. Nonetheless, a well-planned approach, risk management diversification, and a precise knowledge of one's investment horizon and risk tolerance are necessary for successful investing. While those nearing retirement may prioritize safer, income-generating assets, younger people may choose more aggressive investments.

Another crucial component of financial planning is debt management. If not properly managed, debt can be a major financial burden that impedes the achievement of other financial objectives. The urgency and impact of various debt categories, including mortgages, school loans, and credit card debt, differ. If left unchecked, high-interest debt—especially credit card debt—can quickly mount up and become challenging to manage. People should prioritize paying off high-interest debt as soon as feasible while continuing to make regular payments on lower-interest debts as part of their financial strategy. Debt repayment can be accelerated with the use of tactics like the debt avalanche method, which targets high-interest loans, and the debt snowball approach, which concentrates on paying off smaller debts first to create momentum. In addition to providing more money for investments and savings, debt reduction raises one's credit score, which may lead to future chances for better loan terms and cheaper interest rates.

Risk management, a tactic for guarding against unforeseen financial losses, is another component of a comprehensive financial plan. Because it offers a financial safety net in the event of mishaps, illness, or property damage, insurance is essential to risk management. In order to guard against particular dangers, common insurance categories include health, life, car, disability, and homeowners or renters insurance. For instance, health insurance assists in paying for medical bills, while life insurance offers dependents financial support in the event of the policyholder's passing. If an illness or injury prevents a person from working, disability insurance can replace a portion of their income. People can protect their possessions and avoid financial hardship from unforeseen circumstances by carefully choosing the right kinds and amounts of insurance.

In order to ensure a comfortable lifestyle in later years, when income from employment may no longer be available, retirement planning is an essential long-term goal in financial planning. Calculating anticipated expenses, projecting retirement duration, and creating specialized retirement accounts—like an Individual Retirement Account (IRA) or 401(k)—that provide tax benefits to promote long-term saving are all common components of retirement planning. Over time, a sizable retirement fund can be created by making consistent payments to these accounts together with wise investments. Additional income during retirement may also be obtained from employment pensions and Social Security benefits, provided they are available. Inflation, medical expenses, and the intended retirement age are all taken into account in a well-crafted retirement plan. People can experience financial freedom in retirement without worrying about running out of money if they plan ahead and start saving early.

In order to keep the plan current and functional in the face of shifting life circumstances, financial planning also entails ongoing monitoring and recurring revisions. Events in life like getting married, having a kid, changing jobs, or experiencing unforeseen health problems can significantly affect one's financial status. People may adjust to these changes and make sure their financial strategies continue to match their changing objectives and responsibilities by routinely evaluating and revising their financial plans. For instance, it might be feasible to raise retirement contributions or speed up debt repayment when income rises. On the other hand, one may need to temporarily modify savings goals or reduce discretionary spending if financial difficulties occur. Maintaining long-term stability and adjusting to life's difficulties require flexibility in financial planning.

Estate planning, or the process of arranging for the transfer of one's assets after death, is a sometimes disregarded component of financial preparation. In addition to minimizing estate taxes and legal issues for remaining family members, estate planning guarantees that assets are transferred in accordance with one's preferences. Making a will, designating powers of attorney, establishing trusts, and naming beneficiaries are all important components of estate planning. Trusts provide a means of managing and allocating money in a tax-efficient way, specify how assets should be divided and can help avoid disagreements among heirs. If a person becomes incompetent, a power of attorney enables a chosen person to make decisions regarding finances or health care on their behalf. Estate planning is a crucial component of financial preparation for anyone with assets, dependents, or particular desires for the future of their property; it is not just for the wealthy.

As one's financial and personal circumstances change, so does the process of financial planning, which is a lifelong endeavor. Setting goals, budgeting, saving, investing, managing debt, and taking precautions against hazards are all fundamental components of financial planning; nevertheless, the particular tactics and methods must be customized for each person's age, income, family circumstances, and personal beliefs. Early in life, financial planning could be more concerned with developing sound financial habits, conserving money, and investing for growth. The emphasis may change to asset preservation, retirement planning, and homeownership as one moves through different phases of life. Financial planning gives people the ability to make wise decisions, make the most of their financial resources, and feel secure and in charge of their financial future—regardless of age or income.

Beyond the person, family members and even the larger community benefit from financial planning. A properly implemented financial plan can enhance one's general quality of life, ease financial stress, and bring peace of mind. People who are financially prepared are less likely to turn to credit or loans when things are tough, which can cause both financial and emotional stress. Responsible savers and planners are also better able to help family members, make charity contributions, and leave a financial legacy for future generations. By encouraging a culture of accountability and resiliency, financial planning enables people to follow their goals and make contributions to a society that is more financially sound.

Financial planning, a methodical technique that helps people manage their resources efficiently and accomplish their life goals, is essentially the foundation of financial well-being. Financial planning provides a road map for overcoming life's financial obstacles with assurance and direction by taking care of urgent financial requirements, planning for the future, and establishing a solid financial foundation. Financial planning gives you the skills and information you need to create a safe and satisfying financial future, whether you're saving for a milestone, investing for development, or making retirement plans.

Key Components of Financial Planning

A thorough process, financial planning aids people and families in managing their money for long-term security, stability, and prosperity. It entails assessing one's existing financial status, establishing reasonable goals, and creating plans to reach those goals. Financial planning, however, is a continuous process that changes as living circumstances and market conditions do. Effective financial management is complicated and calls for a multifaceted strategy that includes numerous essential elements. Every element has a distinct function and adds to a comprehensive strategy that covers a range of financial health topics. Budgeting, debt management, insurance, risk management, investment planning, retirement planning, tax planning, estate planning, and cash flow management are some of these elements. Anyone hoping to create a financially secure future must comprehend and put each of these components into practice.

Any financial strategy must start with cash flow management since it enables people to monitor their earnings and outlays and regulate their spending patterns. This part entails developing a budget that accounts for both fixed and variable spending and lists monthly income sources. Variable costs, like eating out, entertainment, and shopping, can change, while fixed costs, such as rent, utilities, and insurance payments, never change. Monitoring these expenses is essential for efficient cash flow management in order to make sure that income meets essential costs and leaves space for investments and savings. People can avoid needless debt, gain a better understanding of their financial behaviors, and pinpoint areas for development by managing their cash flow. Furthermore, persistent saving and investing—both of which are necessary for future financial stability and growth—are made possible by effective cash flow management.

Another essential element of financial planning is saving, which acts as a safety net to give people a buffer against unforeseen costs. It is crucial to set aside funds for emergencies since doing so keeps long-term financial plans intact and avoids the need to use credit or loans when things get tough. Although the precise amount may vary based on one's financial status and risk tolerance, an emergency fund should ideally cover three to six months' worth of basic living expenditures. Savings accounts are very liquid, enabling people to access money fast when needed, even though they usually yield lesser returns than investments. In addition to emergency savings, other kinds of savings goals include putting money aside for certain objectives like buying a home, a car, or a trip. People can efficiently manage their finances and prevent using long-term investments when urgent requirements emerge by setting up savings accounts specifically for various objectives.

Since mismanaged debt can impede progress toward reaching financial goals, debt management is an equally important component of financial planning. Interest rates, repayment plans, and the effects on one's financial well-being differ throughout debt categories, including credit card debt, school loans, and mortgages. If not handled wisely, high-interest debt—especially credit card debt—can become crippling since it accumulates over time and lowers discretionary income. Prioritizing payments according to interest rates and balances is part of debt management; this approach reduces total interest costs and speeds up debt repayment. There are a number of ways to pay off debt, such as the debt avalanche and snowball methods. While the debt avalanche technique targets high-interest debt first to lower total interest payments, the debt snowball method concentrates on paying off lesser balances first to generate momentum. People can attain financial stability and enhance their creditworthiness for future borrowing needs by carefully managing their debt, which frees up more of their income for investments and savings.

Another essential component of financial planning is investment planning, which aims to increase wealth over time by allocating funds to a variety of assets such as mutual funds, stocks, bonds, and real estate. Investments seek to produce returns by assuming measured risk, in contrast to savings, which place a higher priority on security and liquidity. Assessing one's risk tolerance, financial objectives, and time horizon is the first step in investment planning because these variables have a big impact on the kinds of investments that are suitable. For instance, younger people may be able to invest more aggressively in stocks or growth-focused funds due to their longer time horizon and better risk tolerance. On the other hand, in order to protect wealth, those who are getting close to retirement might give priority to safer, income-producing investments like bonds or dividend-paying equities. A fundamental idea in investment planning is diversification, which helps distribute risk over several asset classes and lessens the effect of a single investment's underwhelming performance on the portfolio as a whole. Growth and security are balanced in a well-diversified portfolio, which fits a person's risk tolerance and financial goals.

The goal of risk management, a proactive approach to financial planning, is to recognize and reduce risks that could result in losses. Unexpected circumstances, such as disease, accidents, natural catastrophes, or economic downturns, can have serious financial repercussions and affect a person's capacity to reach their financial objectives. One of the main tools for controlling these risks is insurance, which offers a safety net of funds to shield people, families, and property from the expenses of unforeseen circumstances. Health, life, disability, property, and liability insurance are common forms of insurance. For instance, health insurance helps pay for medical bills, preventing personal funds from being depleted by medical demands. While disability insurance replaces income in the event that an individual becomes unable to work due to illness or injury, life insurance offers financial support to dependents in the case of the policyholder's death. People can build a more resilient financial plan and protect themselves and their families from financial distress by choosing the right kinds and amounts of insurance.

Another essential part of financial planning is retirement planning, which makes sure people can continue living the way they want to in retirement without running out of money. Typically, retirement planning entails projecting future spending, figuring out the necessary retirement income, and creating a savings and investment strategy to reach those goals. Because they provide advantages like tax-deferred growth or tax-free withdrawals, tax-advantaged retirement accounts—such as a 401(k), Individual Retirement Account (IRA), or Roth IRA—are useful instruments for building retirement savings. People can gradually accumulate a retirement fund by making regular contributions to these accounts and strategically allocating their assets according to their age and risk tolerance. In addition to personal savings, Social Security benefits and workplace pensions, if available, offer extra income during retirement. Early retirement planning is crucial since compound interest increases long-term growth and enables people to build up a larger retirement fund over time with modest payments. People can become financially independent in retirement and prevent themselves from depending entirely on Social Security or other outside assistance by carefully planning and saving.

A crucial but frequently disregarded component of financial planning is tax planning, which aims to maximize after-tax income and lawfully reduce tax obligations. Understanding the tax ramifications of several financial decisions, including investments, retirement contributions, and property ownership, is essential to effective tax planning. People can lower their taxable income by utilizing tax credits, deductions, and deferrals by making wise decisions. For instance, while contributions to a Roth IRA grow tax-free and can be withdrawn tax-free in retirement, contributions to tax-deferred retirement accounts, such as a standard IRA or 401(k), reduce taxable income in the current year. Holding investments for a long time can also result in tax savings because capital gains on investments kept for more than a year are usually taxed at a lower rate than ordinary income. The tax burden can be further decreased by employing tax-efficient investment techniques such as harvesting tax losses, reducing short-term profits, and using tax-advantaged accounts. An individual's financial well-being can be significantly impacted by comprehending and utilizing tax rules, which enables them to keep a larger portion of their earnings for investing, saving, and other financial objectives.

The act of making arrangements for how one's assets will be distributed after death is known as estate planning. It guarantees that wealth and property are transferred in accordance with one's preferences while reducing tax obligations and legal issues. Anyone with assets, dependents, or specific goals for the future of their property has to plan their estate. Making a will, setting up trusts, naming beneficiaries, and transferring powers of attorney are all important components of estate planning. A will provides clarity on inheritance issues and prevents disagreements among heirs by outlining how a person's possessions should be divided following their passing. Trusts provide people with more choice over how and when recipients get their inheritance, making them a more flexible and tax-efficient way to manage and distribute assets. In the event that a person becomes incapable, powers of attorney appoint somebody to make choices regarding their finances or medical treatment. Planning for estate taxes, which can be necessary if the estate's worth is above specific thresholds, is another aspect of estate planning. People can safeguard their wealth, provide for their loved ones, and leave a financial legacy that represents their goals and values by following these procedures.

When combined, these elements of financial planning offer a comprehensive method of handling finances, guaranteeing that people can meet their present obligations, get ready for their future aspirations, and safeguard themselves from possible financial hazards. Every element is interrelated, and advancement in one field frequently reinforces that in another. Effective budgeting and cash flow management, for instance, lay the groundwork for investments and savings, while risk management and insurance shield accumulated assets against unanticipated losses. Similarly, since tax-advantaged accounts are essential for accumulating retirement funds, retirement and tax planning go hand in hand. Despite being primarily concerned with wealth distribution, estate planning connects to the other elements by guaranteeing that financial choices made during one's lifetime are represented in one's legacy.

Since life events, the state of the economy, and individual objectives all change over time, financial planning is an iterative process that needs constant observation and modification. Significant life events can have a big impact on financial priorities and resources, like getting married, having a kid, changing careers, or experiencing unforeseen health problems. People may adjust to these changes and make sure that their tactics continue to be in line with changing requirements and goals by routinely assessing and revising their financial plans. A young worker, for instance, would place a higher priority on saving and investing heavily, whereas a retiree might prioritize income generation and capital preservation. Because they allow people to face life's uncertainties with resilience and confidence, flexibility and responsiveness are essential.

Beyond a person's financial stability, a thorough financial plan has a positive impact on relationships, job decisions, and even mental health. Anxiety is frequently brought on by financial stress, and a well-thought-out strategy can ease anxiety by outlining precise strategies for reaching financial security. Financial planning also makes it possible for people to follow their goals, whether those goals include starting a business, paying for a child's education, or retiring early. People may take charge of their financial destiny and strive for a life of plenty, fulfillment, and meaning by establishing realistic objectives, laying a solid foundation, and making wise decisions. The main elements of financial planning essentially work as a road map for navigating the intricacies of financial life, enabling people to take charge of their financial destiny and leave a legacy of stability and prosperity for their families.

The Financial Planning Process

The financial planning process is a systematic method that assists people in reaching their financial objectives by following a set of phases that are all intended to address various facets of personal finance. This process entails assessing one's present financial situation, establishing clear goals, creating plans to achieve these goals, putting the strategies into action, and regularly reviewing and modifying the plan as needed. Instead of being a one-time event, financial planning is a process that requires ongoing evaluation and adjustments in response to shifting financial goals, personal circumstances, and economic conditions. People may take charge of their financial destinies, make wise decisions, and lessen the stress that comes with money management by participating in the financial planning process.

Understanding the present financial status is the first stage in the financial planning process. This entails a careful evaluation of one's financial resources, debts, earnings, and outlays. Accurate data collection is necessary to paint a realistic image of one's financial situation and provide a solid basis for further planning stages. Usually, bank statements, tax returns, pay stubs, investment records, loan information, and any information about unpaid debts are used to generate this data. Analyzing cash flow, or the ratio of income to costs reveals a person's spending patterns and shows if they are currently living within or above their means. Knowing these patterns makes it easier to spot areas that may require changes, like cutting back on discretionary spending or boosting revenue. Because it provides a quick overview of one's present financial situation and identifies areas of strength and possible growth, this baseline assessment can be used as a springboard for creating a thorough financial plan.

Setting specific financial goals is the next stage after gaining a thorough awareness of the present financial status. Establishing objectives is essential because it provides focus and direction to the financial strategy. Depending on personal objectives, values, and circumstances, financial goals can be short-, medium-, or long-term and can vary greatly. Short-term objectives, which can usually be accomplished in a year, could be paying off a small debt or creating an emergency fund. With a timeline of one to five years, medium-term objectives could include supporting a significant vacation, buying a car, or saving for a down payment on a home. Long-term objectives, which frequently stretch beyond five years, include saving for retirement, financing children's education, and building wealth for future generations. Every objective necessitates a distinct strategy with differing time horizons, liquidity requirements, and risk tolerance levels. Setting goals also makes prioritizing possible, which aids in efficient resource allocation and helps people steer clear of the pitfalls of pursuing competing goals at the same time. The SMART framework—which states that objectives should be Specific, Measurable, Achievable, Relevant, and Time-bound—is included in a well-defined goal-setting process. This methodical technique enables people to establish reasonable and achievable goals, providing a feeling of achievement and inspiration upon reaching each milestone.

Creating plans to reach the goals that have been set is the next step in the financial planning process. This step entails creating detailed action plans that are suited to each objective while accounting for time constraints, potential hazards, and the resources that are available. A person planning for retirement would give priority to investments with higher yields and tax benefits, such as retirement accounts, but someone looking to save an emergency fund might concentrate on a high-yield savings account. Understanding financial goods and investment possibilities, such as stocks, bonds, mutual funds, real estate, and insurance, which all provide varying degrees of risk and return, is also necessary for developing strategies. By spreading these assets over a variety of asset classes, one can better match the portfolio with their risk tolerance by striking a balance between prospective growth and loss protection. Furthermore, since tax-efficient investing decisions can increase after-tax profits, tax considerations also have a big influence on these techniques. Understanding debt management strategies is also necessary for those who need to pay off high-interest debts before concentrating on their investing objectives. The strategic plan must be thorough, addressing every facet of the person's financial circumstances and providing a clear route forward to accomplish each objective.

After tactics have been established, the financial strategy must be put into action. Since it necessitates constant activity and a dedication to carrying out planned stages, implementation is frequently the most difficult aspect of the process. This stage could entail debt consolidation, frequent transfers to savings accounts, or the setup of automatic contributions to retirement accounts. To ensure that every activity is in line with the overall financial plan, monitoring and tracking progress is also necessary for effective execution. Professional financial advisors can be helpful at this point since they offer advice on how to carry out investment transactions, choose suitable insurance plans, and maximize tax techniques. Advisors can also help people stay accountable by assisting them in making required course corrections and staying on course. However, by adopting digital tools like portfolio management software or budgeting apps to speed up the implementation process, even people who choose a self-directed approach to financial planning can succeed. In the end, a methodical approach to execution generates momentum, turning the financial plan from a conceptual framework into actionable steps that produce quantifiable outcomes.

Following implementation, the plan's performance must be tracked and evaluated on a regular basis. To make sure the plan is applicable and efficient in the face of life changes and market volatility, financial planning is a dynamic process that needs to be reviewed on a regular basis. Financial priorities may need to be adjusted as a result of major life events like marriage, the birth of a child, changing careers, or unforeseen health problems. Investment strategy may also need to be revised in response to economic developments like inflation, interest rate increases, or stock market volatility. People can evaluate their progress toward their goals and make necessary adjustments with the help of regular reviews, which are frequently carried out annually or semiannually. Reviewing cash flow, examining investment and savings balances, and assessing debt levels are all part of monitoring the strategy. This procedure offers a chance to acknowledge accomplishments, pinpoint any areas of concern, and adjust tactics. Regular monitoring guarantees that people continue to manage their money proactively, allowing them to react quickly to changes and stay in line with their objectives.

A crucial component of financial planning is risk management, which protects people against unanticipated circumstances that can impede their financial development. Getting sufficient insurance coverage is one risk management tactic to guard against possible monetary losses due to illness, accidents, property damage, or disability. Each type of insurance—health, life, disability, and property—has a distinct function in safeguarding resources and earnings. For example, disability insurance guarantees income replacement in the event that an individual is unable to work due to illness or accident, while life insurance offers financial support to dependents in the event of the policyholder's death. By helping to pay for medical bills, health insurance keeps savings and investments from being depleted. Emergency funds contribute to risk management in addition to standard insurance by offering money for unforeseen costs without requiring credit. A successful risk management strategy takes into account each person's unique situation when determining the kinds and amounts of insurance required to safeguard their financial stability. People can build a strong financial strategy that can endure life's challenges by carefully managing risk.

Another essential component of financial planning is tax planning, which aims to maximize after-tax returns and reduce tax obligations. Understanding tax regulations, credits, and deductions, as well as how different financial decisions affect taxable income, is necessary for effective tax planning. Depending on the type of account, tax-advantaged accounts, like an Individual Retirement Account (IRA) or 401(k), enable people to either receive tax-free growth or postpone taxes on contributions. Contributions to these accounts lower current taxable income, supporting long-term savings objectives and offering instant tax advantages. Additionally, as assets kept for more than a year are frequently taxed at a lower rate than short-term earnings, capital gains tax concerns influence investment decisions. Tax savings opportunities are created by lowering taxable income through charitable contributions, home mortgage interest deductions, and other tax deductions. These components are integrated into the overall financial plan by a well-rounded tax strategy, which guarantees that tax implications are taken into account in all financial decisions. Tax optimization allows people to keep more of their income, which they can then use for investments, savings, or other financial objectives.

Since retirement planning guarantees financial independence in later life, it is a primary goal for many participants in the financial planning process. Retirement planning is calculating future income requirements, establishing a retirement age, and putting a plan in place to save the required amount of money. To determine a realistic retirement savings goal, factors including inflation, projected lifestyle, and medical costs must be taken into account. Retirement accounts provide tax benefits that increase the growth potential of retirement savings. These include individual plans like IRAs and employer-sponsored plans like 401(k). If offered, employer matching contributions provide workers an extra push and enable them to grow their retirement savings without having to make any more out-of-pocket contributions. Although they are unlikely to cover all costs, Social Security benefits give seniors additional income in addition to their retirement assets. Retirement savings can be increased with diversified investment portfolios that are matched to a person's time horizon and risk tolerance. Early retirement planning enables people to take advantage of compound interest, which facilitates retirement financial independence. People can build a steady income stream that will support their preferred lifestyle in their older years by methodically saving and investing over time.

The last phase of financial planning is estate planning, which makes sure that a person's assets are allocated in accordance with their last desires. To handle the transfer of money, estate planning entails drafting legal papers including a will, trusts, and powers of attorney. By outlining the distribution of assets among beneficiaries, a will helps to avoid disagreements and guarantees that one's objectives are carried out. Additional advantages of trusts include the ability to cut estate taxes, safeguard assets from creditors, and establish terms for asset distribution. Probate court hearings are avoided by designating beneficiaries on investment accounts, life insurance policies, and retirement funds, which expedites the transfer process. Furthermore, in the event that a person becomes incapacitated, powers of attorney appoint people to make financial or medical choices on their behalf. In addition to protecting wealth for future generations, good estate planning supports causes or family members in accordance with the wishes of the individual and is consistent with their values. In order to secure their legacy and provide for their loved ones, estate planning is especially crucial for people with substantial assets, dependents, or philanthropic interests.

Professional advice can be extremely helpful throughout the financial planning process, particularly when navigating intricate financial choices or specialist fields like estate planning, investment management, or tax planning. Financial advisors contribute knowledge and experience, offering unbiased analysis and tailored suggestions. They can assist people in evaluating their existing financial situation, establishing reasonable objectives, creating customized plans, and tracking their progress. In addition to providing accountability, working with an advisor raises the possibility that the financial plan will be followed. When choosing an advisor, people should do their research and take into account things like credentials, expertise, fee schedule, and compatibility with their financial objectives and personal values. A reliable advisor encourages cooperation, enabling customers to reach financial security and make wise judgments.

For anyone looking to attain financial stability, independence, and growth, the financial planning process is a crucial tool. People can take charge of their financial lives and eliminate the uncertainty around money management by evaluating their financial status, establishing specific goals, creating strategies, carrying out and keeping an eye on the plan, and making adjustments as needed. Every step of the procedure, including risk management, tax planning, estate planning, and cash flow analysis, adds to a thorough and flexible strategy for achieving financial success. People are better able to handle financial difficulties, take advantage of opportunities, and strive toward a secure and prosperous future when they fully participate in the financial planning process. This process's discipline, structure, and foresight make it a priceless tool for anyone looking to establish a strong financial foundation and realize their long-term financial goals.

CHAPTER II

Setting Financial Goals

Identifying Your Financial Goals
One of the first steps in financial planning and analysis is determining your financial objectives. This provides a road map that directs all of your income, expenses, savings, investments, and, eventually, financial security. Financial objectives provide direction and purpose to your planning and act as quantifiable benchmarks to monitor your progress. Determining and prioritizing your financial objectives allows you to create a strategic financial plan that fits your ability and aspirations, whether those objectives are to purchase a home, save for retirement, create an emergency fund, or pay for your children's college tuition.

Setting financial goals necessitates self-evaluation, setting priorities, and being clear about both immediate and long-term objectives. Usually attainable in one to three years, short-term financial objectives include saving for a trip, paying off high-interest debt, and creating an emergency fund. However, long-term financial objectives like saving for retirement or purchasing a home typically take ten years or longer to achieve. Because financial security frequently depends on both planning for the future and satisfying immediate needs, striking a balance between both goals is essential. Having a clear idea of your financial objectives promotes a disciplined approach to money management, guarantees sufficient savings, and helps avoid overspending. By defining what really counts, financial objectives help you allocate resources and modify strategies as life circumstances change.

Furthermore, modifying objectives in response to shifting market conditions helps avoid setbacks and enables adaptable strategies that adjust to changes in the economy. For example, it can be wise to temporarily raise cash savings contributions until market stability returns if stock markets are volatile. Your financial planning will stay current and in line with your life if you modify your goals when your personal circumstances—such as getting married, having kids, or changing careers—develop.

Since personal beliefs and lifestyle choices have an impact on saving and spending patterns, setting financial objectives also entails matching them with these choices. For instance, someone who values travel could prioritize saving for trips, while someone who values family might emphasize investing in your kids' education. Setting financial objectives that are in line with your personal values guarantees that they have purpose and inspire you to maintain your discipline. Because you are less likely to give up on goals that have a strong emotional connection, financial plans that align with your values are also more sustainable. For example, if sustainability is a value, you may concentrate on saving for energy-efficient home improvements or investing in socially conscious funds. Long-term success is more likely when you set goals that align with your beliefs and develop a financially satisfying plan.

To stay on course and adjust to changing conditions, financial goals must be reviewed and reassessed on a regular basis. A change in financial priorities is frequently required by life events like a promotion, move, marriage, or the birth of a child. You can make necessary adjustments to timing, spending, and contributions by periodically reviewing your progress toward each target. For instance, you might decide to boost your emergency savings or accelerate payments to your retirement fund if you receive a sizable rise. On the other hand, you might have to temporarily cut back on donations to non-essential goals if you are experiencing financial difficulties. Financial planning that is flexible guarantees that your objectives will continue to be reachable even in the face of unforeseen circumstances.

Since taxes have a big impact on investments and savings, they must be taken into account when identifying and establishing financial goals. You can lower your taxable income and put more money toward long-term objectives by using tax-advantaged accounts like 401(k)s IRAs and Health Savings Accounts (HSAs). You can increase your savings and take advantage of government incentives aimed at promoting financial security by using these accounts. Furthermore, knowing how to minimize the tax burden on assets and maximize profits requires an understanding of capital gains taxes and tax-loss harvesting techniques. Because withdrawals from specific accounts may be taxed differently, tax issues are particularly pertinent when it comes to retirement savings. Effective goal-setting is facilitated by careful tax preparation, which guarantees that you will retain a larger portion of your income while you work toward your goals.

Estate planning, which provides for surviving family members in the case of death or incapacitation, is frequently a part of financial goal-setting. To guarantee that assets are dispersed in accordance with your intentions, estate planning entails naming beneficiaries, establishing trusts, and drafting wills. In order to preserve wealth and lessen the tax burden on heirs, this procedure is essential. To ensure that their financial requirements are satisfied, parents may make provisions in their estate plan for their children's care or education. Having well-defined estate planning also eases the financial and administrative strain on family members at trying times. By including estate planning in your financial objectives, you give people who rely on you a stable legacy that offers continuity and peace of mind.

When setting financial goals, risk management is also crucial because unanticipated circumstances like illness, accidents, or job loss can throw plans for a loop. To guard against monetary loss, risk management entails acquiring the proper insurance coverage, such as health, life, and disability insurance. Sufficient insurance coverage acts as a safety net, preventing unforeseen expenses from using up funds intended for other objectives. In the event of an injury, disability insurance, for example, might replace income, enabling you to keep saving for retirement or other goals. Because it protects their financial security, risk management is especially crucial for families with dependents. Even in the face of unforeseen obstacles, you can continue to make progress toward long-term goals by incorporating insurance into your financial plans.

Since creditworthiness influences your capacity to obtain loans for significant purchases, like a home or car, developing a solid credit history and keeping your credit score high are essential components of financial goal-setting. You can save money over time by obtaining loans with advantageous interest rates if you have good credit. Additionally, more financing alternatives are made available by high credit scores, giving financial planners greater flexibility. Furthermore, prudent credit management keeps you from taking on too much debt, freeing you up to concentrate on your investment and savings objectives. You may improve your credit profile and promote long-term financial stability by routinely checking your credit report and correcting any errors. You can access financial opportunities that help you accomplish important goals by integrating credit management into your financial objectives.

Since investing has the ability to build wealth faster than traditional savings strategies, it is essential for reaching financial goals, especially long-term ones. Investment plans range from conservative options like bonds and dividend stocks to more aggressive options like growth stocks and real estate, depending on the investor's time horizon, goals, and risk tolerance. Investing across a variety of asset classes lowers risk and raises the possibility of consistent returns that help achieve long-term objectives. Since compound interest allows for substantial growth over time, investing is especially crucial for retirement funds. Strategic investment can help you reach your financial objectives more quickly, build wealth, and guarantee financial freedom.

When it comes to setting and reaching financial goals, a dedication to continual learning is crucial because it gives you the information and abilities you need to make wise choices. A thorough grasp of personal finance is provided by financial literacy, which includes risk management, tax planning, investing, and budgeting. Your ability to create reasonable and attainable goals is improved by keeping up with changes in tax legislation, investment opportunities, and economic trends. Additionally, financial education encourages independence, which lessens dependency on experts and makes proactive money management possible. For instance, you can optimize your savings on your own by learning about investment methods and retirement accounts. Making financial education a top priority gives you the ability to make wise financial decisions that advance your long-term objectives.

Lastly, setting financial objectives necessitates perseverance and patience because reaching them frequently calls for sacrifices, focused work, and disappointments. Financial goal-setting frequently involves delayed satisfaction because funds are allocated to investments and savings rather than instant spending. Long-term motivation maintenance can be difficult, especially in the face of monetary difficulties or market instability. Persistence is encouraged, though, when you have a firm focus on your objectives and the advantages they provide. Reminding you of your progress and celebrating little victories along the way, like paying off a credit card or hitting a savings goal, helps you keep moving forward. Financial success is rarely achieved overnight; rather, it takes time and constant, disciplined action.

To sum up, setting financial objectives is a thorough process that calls for introspection, preparation, and flexibility. Every stage of creating a comprehensive and successful financial plan, from evaluating needs and establishing SMART goals to integrating risk management, tax strategies, and lifetime financial education, is important. Financial objectives act as a compass, pointing you in the direction of stability, independence, and financial security. You may develop a financial plan that aligns with your beliefs, equips you to handle unforeseen circumstances, and enables you to have a satisfying life by carefully determining and prioritizing these objectives. Your financial objectives should change along with your priorities and circumstances to keep your financial plan robust, current, and in line with your long-term vision.

Prioritizing and Balancing Goals

In the intricate process of financial planning and analysis, setting priorities and striking a balance between financial objectives is crucial. Building an emergency fund, paying off debt, saving for retirement, investing, financing school, and making plans for major life events like home ownership or having a family are just a few of the many goals that fall under the umbrella of financial goals. Individuals and families must allocate their income and assets toward these goals in a way that maximizes financial stability and satisfies both short-term and long- term requirements because of limited resources and an unpredictable economic climate. To create a balanced and long-lasting financial plan, financial planning and analysis entail ranking these objectives according to urgency, risk, potential return on investment, and personal values.

Knowing the difference between necessities and wants is a fundamental component of setting financial goals in order of importance. A thorough evaluation of basic necessities that are necessary for daily life, such as housing, food, healthcare, and transportation, is frequently the first step in financial planning. Since needs provide stability and security, they must take precedence over discretionary spending. Contrarily, wants are lifestyle decisions or improvements that may raise one's standard of living but are not necessary for survival, such as eating out, taking a trip, or purchasing luxuries. People can make sure that necessities are paid for first and prevent financial stress that could result from spending too much on discretionary items by making a clear distinction between requirements and wants. By putting needs before wants, people can also establish a solid financial foundation that allows them to pursue other financial objectives without jeopardizing stability.

Setting SMART goals—specific, measurable, realistic, relevant, and time-bound—is another essential component of prioritizing financial objectives. Goals become clearer when the SMART framework is used, which makes it simpler to prioritize and monitor them over time. For example, rephrasing a vague objective like "save money for retirement" to "save $500,000 for retirement by age 65 through monthly contributions and investments" makes it more actionable. The SMART approach's specificity guarantees that objectives are reasonable and based on a person's financial situation. It is simpler to determine which goals should be prioritized according to time frame, importance, and feasibility when each goal is well-defined. Establishing SMART goals also enables frequent progress reports, which assist people in modifying their financial plans in reaction to changes in their lives or the state of the economy.

Since emergency funds offer a vital safety net in the event of unforeseen expenses, such as large house repairs, medical emergencies, or job loss, they are frequently among the most important financial objectives. Building an emergency fund equal to three to six months' worth of living expenses is often advised by financial experts since it usually offers sufficient coverage for unforeseen events without the need for high-interest debt. Establishing an emergency fund is essential because it safeguards other financial objectives. For instance, without one, a person may have to take money out of retirement savings or take on debt to pay for unforeseen expenses, which would impede their progress toward other objectives. Setting up money for emergencies strengthens financial resilience and lowers the chance of financial setbacks, allowing people to stay focused on long-term goals.

Repayment of debt, especially high-interest debt, is another crucial financial planning concern. Due to high interest rates, debt—particularly from credit cards, personal loans, or payday loans—can mount up quickly, undermining financial stability and preventing the achievement of other objectives. Making debt repayment a top priority reduces the effects of compound interest, which ultimately saves money and frees up income for investments and savings. For instance, paying off a $10,000 credit card debt with a 20% interest rate quickly could save hundreds or even thousands of dollars as opposed to paying it off gradually over time. In addition to alleviating financial hardship, those who get rid of high-interest debt have more money available for wealth-building endeavors like retirement investments and other long-term objectives. Prioritizing debt repayment also promotes a disciplined attitude to money management, which lessens reliance on borrowed cash and promotes healthier spending practices.

After paying off high-interest debt, emergency expenses, and necessities, people can start directing their resources toward longer-term objectives like retirement savings. Achieving retirement planning is a major financial objective that usually takes decades of steady contributions. Most people make saving for retirement a top priority because of the exponential increase that can result from early and regular contributions due to the power of compound interest. Matching contributions are frequently included in employer-sponsored retirement accounts, such as 401(k) in the U.S., which encourage people to prioritize saving for retirement. People can lower their taxable income, accumulate wealth, and improve their retirement financial security by making the most of their contributions to tax-advantaged accounts. The advantage of starting retirement savings early in one's employment is that it gives investments more time to develop over time with less intensive contributions than if one were to start later in life.

People frequently shift their attention to medium-term objectives, like buying a home, paying for school, or investing in a business, after building a foundation with emergency reserves, debt reduction, and retirement savings. Since these objectives usually include substantial costs that can have a substantial influence on cash flow, careful planning is necessary. For instance, purchasing a home frequently entails paying for a down payment, closing charges, and continuing maintenance in addition to the purchase price. Understanding the entire financial commitment and determining if it fits with one's budget and long-term plans are necessary to balance homeownership with other financial objectives. In the same way, saving for education, whether for oneself or one's children, can be a significant cost that calls for early and regular savings. Dedicated accounts, like the U.S. 529 plan for education, which provides tax benefits for college savings, are frequently used when planning for these objectives. Setting medium-term objectives in order of importance according to their potential return on investment and compatibility with one's personal values aids in the development of a well-rounded financial plan that takes care of current obligations without compromising long-term objectives.

Evaluating and controlling risk is another aspect of balancing objectives in financial planning. The risk associated with various financial objectives varies, and setting priorities frequently necessitates taking one's time horizon and risk tolerance into account. For example, low-risk, easily accessible accounts, like savings accounts, are usually used when saving for a short-term objective, like a vacation. On the other hand, retirement planning, which has a longer time horizon, may include riskier investments like equities, which could yield higher returns. People can create a balanced portfolio that supports both short-term liquidity and long-term growth by diversifying their investments according to time horizon and risk tolerance. For objectives that demand stability, like emergency savings, which should be kept in low-risk, highly liquid accounts to guarantee money is there when needed, risk management is especially crucial. By distributing risk among several objectives, one can lessen the effect of market fluctuations on the overall financial strategy and make steady progress toward each goal.

Setting priorities and balancing financial objectives are significantly impacted by tax concerns. A variety of account types, including health savings accounts (HSAs), education savings plans, and retirement funds, provide tax benefits that can increase savings and lower taxable income. Traditional 401(k) and IRA contributions, for instance, are frequently tax deductible, reducing taxable income in the current year. In contrast, Roth IRAs provide tax-free growth, which makes them appealing for long-term investing. Accessible to individuals with high-deductible health plans, health savings accounts offer triple tax benefits: tax deductions for contributions, tax-free growth on gains, and tax-free withdrawals for approved medical costs. People can increase the effectiveness of their investments and savings by utilizing these tax-advantaged accounts, allocating more funds to their financial objectives. Enhancing overall financial stability, making sure that resources are spent efficiently, and promoting a balanced financial plan are all made possible by being aware of tax consequences and giving priority to goals that have tax benefits.

A key component of keeping a financial plan balanced is routinely evaluating and modifying financial objectives. Events like marriage, having a kid, changing careers, or economic downturns cause life circumstances and financial priorities to alter over time. People can adjust to these changes by reevaluating their financial goals on a regular basis, reordering their priorities, and reallocating resources as necessary. For example, if interest rates are favorable, a couple who intends to purchase a home might decide to boost their payments to the down payment fund, whereas someone who has unforeseen medical expenditures might need to concentrate more on emergency savings. By modifying objectives in response to evolving conditions, the financial plan is kept current, practical, and able to satisfy both short-term and long-term demands. Because it enables people to react proactively to life changes without impeding the pursuit of other objectives, this flexibility is essential for reaching financial stability.

Since investing allows for the building of wealth that can outweigh the constraints of savings alone, it is essential for balancing financial goals, particularly long-term ones. Aligning asset allocation with each financial goal's time horizon and risk tolerance is a key component of effective investment strategies. While short-term objectives, like saving for a down payment on a home, may call for safer, lower-volatility assets like bonds or money market funds, retirement savings, which may have a several-decade time horizon, may require a more aggressive investment strategy with a larger percentage in stocks. Additionally, diversification across asset classes reduces risk by offering a well-rounded strategy that guards against market downturns and promotes consistent growth. People can balance risk and return and move closer to long-term financial security by carefully choosing assets that fit their objectives.

Finally, promoting financial literacy is a continuous objective that improves the capacity to successfully prioritize and balance other financial objectives. Budgeting, investing, tax planning, risk management, and retirement planning are all included in financial literacy. Strong financial knowledge enables people to avoid typical financial errors, adjust to changes in the economy, and make well-informed decisions. People who have received financial education are better equipped to manage their money by setting reasonable objectives, making the most of their investments, and making necessary corrections. People can make proactive decisions that promote balanced financial growth by keeping up with market circumstances, regulatory changes, and financial trends. People who prioritize financial literacy develop a foundation of knowledge that, in the long run, facilitates prudent goal-setting and effective financial planning.

In summary, setting priorities and striking a balance between financial objectives in financial planning and analysis is a complex process that calls for a thorough evaluation of needs, wants, time horizon, risk tolerance, tax ramifications, and individual values. People may effectively distribute resources and guarantee that both immediate needs and long-term ambitions are satisfied by defining specific, attainable goals and creating a hierarchy based on priority and urgency. In addition to prudent debt management and investment management, balancing financial objectives also entails bolstering resilience with emergency savings and insurance. Maintaining the financial plan's alignment with changing priorities is further ensured by routinely assessing and modifying financial goals in light of life events and the state of the economy. In the end, a well-rounded approach to financial planning helps people build a stable and sustainable financial future without compromising their sense of purpose.

SMART Financial Goals

Effective financial planning and analysis are based on SMART financial goals, which provide a framework for people and organizations to make reasonable and doable plans for their financial future. The SMART framework, which stands for Specific, Measurable, Achievable, Relevant, and Time-bound, provides an organized method for establishing objectives that are precise, targeted, and focused on measurable outcomes. SMART financial goals give financial planning direction and clarity by empowering people to deconstruct difficult goals into achievable steps that result in significant advancement. Individuals and organizations can create a strategic approach to financial management, progress monitoring, and situational adaptation by applying the SMART criteria to financial goals.

Specificity, the first element of SMART financial goals, necessitates a thorough explanation of one's objectives. Establishing precise financial goals removes uncertainty, gives a clear picture of the aim, and lowers the possibility of distraction or confusion. For instance, "save $10,000 for an emergency fund within the next 12 months" would be a specific objective rather than a general one like "save more money." This degree of detail specifies the goal of the savings, the precise amount required, and the timeline for achieving it. It is simpler to create a plan to accomplish goals that are defined because they give direction. Specificity is essential in financial planning since it helps to match objectives with each person's unique needs, circumstances, and goals. People can more effectively allocate resources, recognize possible obstacles, and lay out the procedures needed to achieve each goal by clearly outlining their goals.

Measurability, or setting criteria to monitor progress toward the goal, is the second component of SMART financial goals. Quantitative components that clearly show progress, like precise numbers, percentages, or milestones, are incorporated into measurable goals. For example, if the aim is to save $10,000 in a year, the person can monitor achievement gradually by dividing it down into monthly targets of about $833. This method of goal-setting enables frequent evaluations, enabling one to ascertain whether they are ahead, behind, or on track. Because it provides a foundation for accountability and motivation, measurability is very useful in financial planning and analysis. Setting quantifiable goals allows people to objectively assess their progress, which can be particularly inspiring when they observe small gains. Furthermore, quantifiable goals allow people to spot any differences between their performance and their plan, which leads to changes to stay on course with the end aim. Measurability essentially turns a financial objective from an ideal into a tangible goal that can be methodically pursued and assessed.

The third pillar of SMART financial goals is achievable, which highlights the significance of establishing reasonable and reachable goals. Setting goals that are too difficult or unrealistic can cause irritation, discouragement, and, eventually, goal abandonment, even though ambitious goals can be motivating. A person's income, expenses, resources, and present financial status are all taken into account while setting attainable financial objectives. To save $50,000 in a year, for example, might be too ambitious for someone with a moderate income and a large amount of debt already in place. Based on a thorough examination of monthly income and expenses, a more achievable objective may be to save $5,000 to $10,000 in the same time period. Achievability increases the likelihood that goals will be achieved by ensuring that they are appropriate for one's financial situation. Since they shed light on spending trends, debt commitments, and income stability, financial planning and analysis are essential to determining achievability. Setting attainable goals helps people stay motivated, gain financial confidence, and provide the groundwork for bigger future ambitions.

The SMART framework's fourth criterion, "the relevance of financial goals," emphasizes the significance of establishing goals that are in line with one's personal values and larger financial ambitions. Relevant financial goals are significant, represent the priorities that are most important to the person or organization, and enhance overall financial well-being. For instance, someone who desires financial stability in their later years could wish to prepare for retirement, whereas someone who wants immediate financial stability might want to construct an emergency fund. Relevance makes financial objectives more powerful and inspiring by ensuring that they are linked to a greater cause rather than being random. This part of goal-setting pushes people to consider each goal's significance in relation to their financial strategy and life goals. By concentrating on pertinent objectives, people can steer their efforts toward goals that support their preferred lifestyle, future aspirations, and financial freedom rather than squandering money on endeavors that might not contribute to long-term financial health.

The time-bound element, which entails establishing a precise date for accomplishing each target, is the last part of SMART's financial goals. Time-bound goals provide people with structure and a sense of urgency, which motivates them to consistently work toward their goals. Establishing due dates aids in task prioritization, procrastination avoidance, and goal concentration. For instance, if the objective is to pay off $5,000 in credit card debt, setting a 12-month time period makes it obvious when monthly payments are due, which promotes frugal spending and budgeting. In financial planning and analysis, time-bound objectives are especially crucial since they provide a foundation for resource scheduling and budgeting. People are more inclined to plan proactively and look for ways to maximize their income and spending in order to reach financial goals within the allotted time frame when they have deadlines. Because SMART goals are time-bound, they also make it easier to conduct periodic reviews, which enables people to modify their plans in light of their progress and any unanticipated events.

The process of financial planning and analysis is transformed when the SMART framework is applied to financial goals; it becomes organized, useful, and results-oriented. SMART financial goals help people create a roadmap that leads to measurable results by guiding them in the development of concrete steps. An example of a SMART goal would be to "save $30,000 for a home down payment within three years by allocating $833 per month from income and investment returns" for a family looking to save for a down payment on a house. The family can monitor their progress, make any adjustments to their savings plan, and stay motivated as they grow closer to becoming homeowners thanks to this SMART objective, which offers clear direction, a realistic time period, and a measurable target. People are better able to balance short-term and long-term demands, manage conflicting priorities, and steer clear of the traps associated with ambiguous or unrealistic goal-setting when they use SMART goals in their financial planning.

The capacity of SMART financial goals to be adjusted to changing conditions is one of its main advantages. Life events, the state of the economy, and individual objectives all change over time, so financial planning and analysis are not static. Because goals can be changed, rearranged, or reordered as necessary, the SMART framework provides flexibility. For instance, if a person receives a raise in income as a result of a work promotion, they can decide to boost their retirement contributions or save more quickly, or they might decide to take on new financial goals like investing in further education. On the other hand, people might temporarily modify their objectives to meet the urgent demand in the event of an unforeseen expense, such as a medical emergency. Because the SMART approach promotes ongoing evaluation and recalibration, people can continue to be adaptable to changes while remaining dedicated to their financial goals. Because of their adaptability, SMART goals are especially useful for long-term financial planning since they can be adjusted to account for life's unforeseen events without affecting the main course of the financial plan.

Because they motivate people to take deliberate action toward their goals, SMART financial goals also support financial discipline. By offering a methodical framework for goal-setting, the SMART criteria assist people in avoiding rash financial choices that can compromise their advancement. For example, setting a SMART goal to "save $5,000 within eight months by reducing discretionary spending and increasing monthly contributions" while saving for a big purchase, like a new car or vacation, promotes frugal spending practices. People are less likely to spend money on pointless things when they have a defined target and a workable plan because they know how it will affect their main objective. This practice carries over into other facets of financial planning, such as investment strategies, retirement savings, and debt management, where SMART goals help people make deliberate, consistent decisions that support their financial goals.

The effect that SMART financial goals have on empowerment and financial confidence is another benefit. Reaching financial objectives, no matter how little creates a feeling of achievement and boosts self-assurance in one's capacity for sound money management. Successfully paying off a credit card load or setting aside money for emergencies, for instance, gives people a sense of resilience and control that inspires them to aim higher with their financial goals. Financial goals appear less intimidating when they are broken down into manageable components that can be addressed one step at a time, thanks to the SMART framework's emphasis on specificity, measurability, and achievability. As people reach their financial objectives, they get important experience in investing, saving, and budgeting, which makes them more informed and confident in their financial judgment. This increased self-assurance is a strong motivator that encourages people to pursue bigger financial objectives and keep moving forward on their path to financial freedom.

Beyond personal finance, SMART goals are used in business financial planning and analysis to assist firms in establishing and achieving financial goals that promote expansion and profitability. Targets for revenue growth, cost reduction, profitability, or investment in new projects are examples of SMART financial goals in a corporate setting. For example, a company may decide to "increase revenue by 15% within the next fiscal year by expanding the customer base through targeted marketing campaigns" using SMART goals. Businesses may monitor performance, allocate resources efficiently, and make data-driven decisions to support their goals by setting clear, quantifiable, and time-bound goals. In company financial planning, SMART goals are particularly helpful since they make sure that financial operations support long-term growth and competitive advantage by coordinating the organization's financial strategy with its overarching mission and long-term vision.

SMART financial objectives are a useful tool for people who want to better grasp financial concepts in the larger framework of financial literacy. Setting SMART objectives necessitates familiarity with fundamental financial ideas like compound growth, interest rates, investment returns, and budgeting. People strengthen their financial knowledge and skills by gaining practical experience with these concepts as they work toward their SMART goals. For people who are new to financial planning, this instructional component of SMART objectives is very helpful because it offers a practical learning experience. People who establish and meet SMART financial goals get a deeper comprehension of financial planning and analysis over time, which enables them to advocate for their financial well-being and make wise decisions.

To sum up, SMART financial goals offer an organized method for establishing, pursuing, and accomplishing financial goals, making them an effective tool in financial planning and analysis. Specificity, measurability, achievability, relevance, and time-bound deadlines are the key components of the SMART framework, which turns nebulous goals into workable programs that yield measurable outcomes. By encouraging resilience, confidence, and financial discipline, SMART goals help people efficiently manage their money and adjust to shifting conditions. SMART goals help with risk management, long-term strategic planning, and effective resource allocation in both personal and commercial finance. In addition to improving financial literacy, SMART objectives' educational advantages enable people and families to accumulate wealth, become financially independent, and establish long-term financial security. Individuals and organizations may take charge of their financial destinies and get steadily closer to a stable and prosperous life by adopting SMART financial goals.

CHAPTER III

Building a Budget

Basics of Budgeting

A key component of financial planning and analysis is budgeting, which acts as a road map for people and organizations to allocate resources, manage their money wisely, and work toward both immediate and long-term financial objectives. Fundamentally, budgeting is the process of making a spending and saving plan that enables people to monitor their earnings, outlays, and financial development over time. Good budgeting gives financial decision-making a framework, which facilitates debt reduction, expenditure management, and future savings. This crucial talent enables people to attain financial security, lessen financial strain, and keep command of their financial lives. Budgeting is equally important for organizations since it directs financial projections, resource allocation, and operational decision-making. Understanding revenue and expenses, classifying and prioritizing spending, and routinely reviewing and modifying the budget to accommodate evolving needs are all part of the foundations of budgeting.

Understanding income, which is the entire amount of money received from different sources like wages, investments, or business profits, is the first step in creating a budget. Setting reasonable spending and savings targets and determining one's total financial capabilities depend on an accurate income calculation. While income for businesses is made up of revenue from the sale of goods or services as well as additional sources like investment earnings, income for people usually comes from work, side occupations, rental income, or investment returns. Since total income represents the amount of money available for saving and paying bills, it provides a clear beginning point for budgeting. Since it represents the real cash flow available after deductions for things like taxes, insurance, and retirement contributions, after-tax income, also known as net income, is crucial for creating a budget. This helps avoid overpaying and guarantees that the budget is based on reasonable numbers.

The next essential step in creating a budget is to comprehend spending. The money that must be spent on living expenses, debt repayment, and other commitments is known as expenses. There are two types of expenses: fixed and variable. Regular, predictable costs that don't fluctuate from month to month are known as fixed expenses. Examples of these include rent or mortgage payments, auto payments, and insurance premiums. On the other hand, variable costs—such as food, entertainment, utilities, and eating out—vary according to usage and lifestyle decisions. Making the distinction between these two categories of expenses enables people to pinpoint areas in which their spending is flexible and under their control. For example, variable expenses allow for modifications and savings, whereas fixed expenses must be reported monthly. To create a balanced budget that takes into consideration both necessary and discretionary spending, it is crucial to comprehend the type and frequency of expenses.

Developing a spending plan, which distributes revenue across several expense categories, is a fundamental component of budgeting. While allowing for savings and discretionary expenditure, a well-organized spending plan guarantees that necessary costs are met. People can start by enumerating all of their essential costs and allocating a certain percentage of their income to each one in order to develop a spending plan. For instance, one of the biggest expenses and one that might take up a huge amount of the budget is housing costs, such as rent or mortgage payments. Transportation, groceries, utilities, and healthcare may be additional crucial areas. Although they often receive a smaller allotment, discretionary categories like entertainment and eating out are also covered. People may get a clear view of how their money is being spent and make sure that all of their basic necessities are satisfied before putting money into discretionary expenditure by dividing their income into different categories. The spending plan is an effective tool for financial management since it establishes limits for every area, assisting people in avoiding impulsive or excessive spending that can put a strain on their finances.

Building financial security and accomplishing long-term objectives require saving, which is a crucial part of budgeting. By setting aside a part of income for savings, a well-designed budget enables people to save for unexpected expenses, make investments in potential future opportunities, and progress toward financial independence. The "pay yourself first" idea, which entails putting aside a part of income for savings before paying for other obligations, is frequently advised by financial gurus. By treating savings as an unavoidable expense, this strategy makes sure that people continuously strive toward their financial objectives. Depending on the time horizon and goal, savings can be categorized into various types, including emergency funds, retirement savings, and savings for particular objectives like buying a home or paying for school. An emergency fund is especially crucial since it acts as a safety net for unforeseen costs like auto repairs or medical expenditures, minimizing the need for credit cards or loans during emergencies. One of the most effective steps to long-term stability and financial resilience is developing a strong saving habit within a budget.

Another essential component of budgeting is debt management. Debt is a major burden for many people, limiting their capacity to save and spend as they like. People can lower their total debt load, raise their credit score, and eventually become financially independent by making debt payback a priority in their budget. When creating a debt budget, it's critical to take into account the several kinds of debt, including credit card debt, school loans, auto loans, and mortgages, as well as the interest rates associated with each. Credit card balances and other high-interest debt frequently need to be paid off right away since interest may mount up quickly and become a significant financial burden. Techniques like the debt avalanche or snowball approaches may be used when creating a budget for debt repayment. While the debt avalanche approach targets high-interest debt to lower overall interest expenses, the debt snowball method concentrates on paying off smaller accounts first to obtain a psychological boost. People can methodically lower their debt load and free up money for savings and other financial objectives by including debt repayment in their budget.

A key component of effective budgeting is keeping track of spending since it enables people to keep an eye on their spending patterns, spot areas where they are going over budget, and make sure they are remaining within it. Frequent expense tracking reveals whether the budgeted amounts are sustainable and reasonable by shedding light on real spending trends. Spreadsheets, written cost logs, and budgeting applications are just a few of the tools and techniques available for tracking spending. These tools assist people in keeping track of their transactions, classifying their spending, and comparing their actual and planned spending. Consistent cost tracking is crucial for accountability because it draws attention to any differences between actual and planned spending. People can spot patterns in this data, such as excessive spending in particular areas, and modify their budgets accordingly. In addition to helping you remain on course, tracking your expenses is a great way to gather data that can help you make better budgeting decisions in the future.

Promoting financial discipline and lowering the probability of impulsive or unexpected spending are two of the main advantages of budgeting. A well-structured budget gives people a clear framework for making decisions and enables them to prioritize their expenditures according to their values and financial objectives. For example, if eating out is a discretionary expense, the budget can set aside a certain amount each month for this category to keep spending under control. By helping people distinguish between needs and wants, budgeting makes it simpler to steer clear of pointless expenditures that could jeopardize their financial progress. People are more likely to make prudent spending decisions that support their overall financial goals when they follow a budget. Long-term financial success is mostly dependent on the discipline that budgeting cultivates since it promotes self-control, intentionality, and a responsible mindset.

Establishing financial objectives gives the budgeting process focus and a sense of purpose. There are many different types of financial goals, from short-term ones like saving for a trip to long-term ones like retirement planning. Setting specific financial objectives helps people budget by relating their everyday financial choices to their larger ambitions. As progress is accomplished over time, goals offer inspiration and a feeling of accomplishment. Financial objectives can be prioritized and resources allocated appropriately within a budget, guaranteeing that they continue to be a primary emphasis. For example, the budget might set aside a specific portion of income each month for retirement accounts if saving for retirement is a high priority. People can develop a dynamic plan that supports their long-term financial vision while simultaneously meeting their immediate requirements by integrating goals into the budgeting process.

In order to stay effective, budgeting needs to be monitored and adjusted on a regular basis. The budget frequently needs to be revised as needs, ambitions, and financial situations change over time. For instance, one's capacity to save money or cover expenses may be greatly impacted by a change in income, such as a rise or a job loss. Similar to this, life events like getting married, starting a family, or purchasing a home come with additional financial obligations that could need modifying the budget. People can evaluate their progress, make the required adjustments, and maintain alignment with their financial objectives by reviewing the budget on a regular basis. The budget is kept current and flexible to changing conditions through this review and adjustment process, which keeps it from becoming out-of-date or ineffectual. People may keep financial control and confidently handle opportunities and difficulties by approaching budgeting as a dynamic process.

Effective resource allocation, cash flow management, and financial sustainability are all made possible by budgeting, which is a fundamental component of financial planning and analysis for firms. Revenue forecasts, operating costs, capital expenditures, and profit targets are frequently included in business budgets. Management may make well-informed decisions on investments, cost control, and strategic objectives with the help of a well-crafted business budget, which offers a roadmap for growth and profitability. Setting financial goals, like increasing income or cutting expenses, and monitoring performance in relation to these goals are other components of business budgeting. An organization's financial responsibility, transparency, and effective use of its resources all depend on this budgeting and analysis process. Businesses can reduce financial risks, maintain operational consistency, and set themselves up for long-term success by sticking to a budget.

Budgeting has significant psychological advantages as well because it gives one a sense of control, lowers financial worry, and increases confidence in one's capacity for money management. Many people suffer from stress brought on by debt, unclear finances, or insufficient savings, which can have a detrimental effect on their general well-being. By providing a clear financial management plan that enables people to make wise decisions and steer clear of financial hazards, budgeting helps people cope with some of this stress. Because they have a plan in place to manage their debt, save for the future, and handle their costs, people who budget feel more safe and prepared. A proactive attitude to financial health and a positive connection with money are fostered by this empowering sense of control. By establishing specific financial goals, keeping an eye on cash flow, and spotting possible hazards, budgeting helps organizations lower financial uncertainty. Budgeting's discipline and structure help create a stable financial climate that fosters innovation, development, and organizational resilience.

Budgeting is a potent instrument in the context of financial planning and analysis that helps people and organizations make strategic decisions, maximize their financial resources, and strive toward worthwhile objectives. A foundation for financial discipline is provided by budgeting, which enables people to track their progress, adjust to changes, and distribute resources according to priorities. It encourages deliberate spending and regular saving by cultivating an intentional mentality. Through careful planning and resource management, budgeting supports growth and profitability for firms and ensures financial stability. The fundamentals of budgeting set the stage for financial success, enabling both individuals and businesses to prosper in a cutthroat market. Budgeting is an essential skill that helps ensure a stable, robust, and prosperous financial future, whether one is managing personal finances or an enterprise.

Creating a Sustainable Budget

A key component of financial planning and analysis is developing a sustainable budget, which gives people and organizations a methodical way to handle their money over time. A sustainable budget is one that can be regularly followed without leading to excessive debt, financial strain, or an unsustainable way of living. It necessitates striking a balance between income and costs, making thoughtful decisions about spending and saving that are in line with one's own or an organization's beliefs and objectives, and planning for both predictable and unforeseen financial occurrences. In order to achieve financial stability and security, creating a sustainable budget entails more than just keeping track of spending; it also entails developing financial discipline, adjusting to life changes, and making ongoing adjustments. Achieving long-term financial health in the complicated economic climate of today requires creating a flexible and resilient budget.

Assessing and comprehending revenue is a fundamental step in developing a sustainable budget, as it forms the cornerstone of all financial planning. Income is the total amount of money that a person or organization makes, usually on a monthly or yearly basis. It can come from a variety of sources, including business income, bonuses, investments, and salaries. Setting reasonable spending and saving goals is aided by having a precise picture of income. The amount that remains after taxes, insurance, and other deductions is known as net income or take-home pay, and it is crucial for individuals to take this into account. A clearer picture of what is affordable within the budget is provided by net income, which represents the real amount of money available for spending and saving. With revenue streams originating from several sources, revenues for businesses may be more complicated. To determine the overall financial capability, these sources need to be closely monitored and averaged, particularly if income varies seasonally or on a monthly basis. To guarantee that all costs and financial goals are in line with what is actually available, creating a sustainable budget necessitates beginning with a realistic assessment of revenue.

Another essential component of a sustainable budget is comprehending and classifying spending. There are two types of expenses: fixed costs and variable costs. Rent, mortgage payments, insurance premiums, and loan payments are examples of fixed expenses that don't vary each month. Usually non-negotiable, these need to be addressed in order to preserve fundamental stability. Conversely, variable costs—such as food, eating out, entertainment, and energy bills—vary according to consumption and lifestyle decisions. By recognizing and classifying these costs, one can better analyze spending trends and make the necessary modifications to establish a sustainable and balanced budget. It enables people and organizations to differentiate between discretionary costs that can be changed in accordance with financial priorities and goals and essential costs that are required for fundamental operations. For example, if other financial objectives, like setting up money for an emergency fund, are given priority, the amount spent on eating out can be changed or reduced, even though rent is a fixed and necessary expense. People can create a budget that fits their goals and budgetary constraints by strategically deciding where to reallocate resources or make cuts after accurately recognizing expenses.

Instead of considering savings as an afterthought, an efficient, sustainable budget makes it a top priority. Particularly when faced with unforeseen costs or economic uncertainties, savings offer a financial buffer that promotes long-term security and resilience. The "pay yourself first" strategy, which entails reserving a part of income for savings before distributing funds to other expenses, is one suggested method. By making saving a regular habit, this strategy fosters financial security and independence. Based on objectives and time horizons, savings can be categorized into a number of different areas, such as short-term savings for urgent needs, an emergency fund for unforeseen costs, long-term savings for retirement, or important future objectives like buying a home or paying for school. An emergency fund is especially crucial since it acts as a safety net against unforeseen costs like auto repairs, medical bills, or unexpected income loss, which lessens the need for credit or loans. A realistic savings strategy that takes both immediate and long-term demands into account is essential to a healthy budget. Regularly setting aside a percentage of income helps people become more resilient and ready for life's unexpected obstacles, keeping them from being thrown off course by financial crises.

Another important component of developing a sustainable budget is debt management. Overspending can impede financial advancement and restrict savings, making it challenging to meet long-term financial objectives. A sustainable budget outlines a strategy for managing debt repayment, with an emphasis on lowering high-interest debt initially to reduce interest payments over time. The debt avalanche approach, which targets high-interest debt to lower overall expenses, and the debt snowball method, which emphasizes paying off lesser balances first for psychological incentive, are two tactics for debt repayment. People who regularly set aside a percentage of their income for debt repayment can progressively lower their debt load and free up money for other important expenses. In addition to enhancing financial stability, budget-friendly debt management raises credit scores, which can lead to better lending conditions, cheaper interest rates, and more financial flexibility. A budget must take into account debt as a continuous expense and include plans for gradually lowering it in order to be genuinely sustainable. With this strategy, people and organizations may take back financial control and strive toward debt freedom.

The flexibility to adjust to shifting conditions is one of the hallmarks of a sustainable budget. Because life is unpredictable, priorities and financial demands may change over time as a result of things like unanticipated emergencies, work changes, family needs, and economic situations. A sustainable budget may adapt to these changes without putting a heavy financial burden on the budget. A sustainable budget, for instance, enables prompt modifications to discretionary expenditure in the event of a decline in income, reallocating funds to cover necessary needs and reducing the impact on savings. On the other hand, a sustainable budget can help people take advantage of advantageous financial times by adding additional objectives or increasing savings contributions if income rises. Maintaining the budget's relevance to the requirements and conditions of the present requires regular reviews and adjustments. Given how quickly company environments can change and affect income, expenses, and strategic priorities, this flexibility is particularly crucial for financial planning in businesses. Individuals and organizations can respond proactively to changes and preserve financial stability even during difficult times by including flexibility in the budgeting process.

Setting reasonable goals is another essential component of developing a sustainable budget. In budgeting, goals are crucial for giving direction and inspiration, but they also need to be attainable given the resources at hand. To make sure they are realistic and in line with the budget, financial goals should be SMART (specific, measurable, achievable, relevant, and time-bound). An example of a particular aim might be "saving $200 per month for an emergency fund over the next 12 months," as opposed to the more general one of "saving more money." Because too ambitious goals might cause discouragement if they are impossible to achieve, setting realistic goals within the budget helps avoid frustration and fatigue. Realistic goals also aid in keeping financial development moving at a steady rate, enabling people and organizations to accumulate money, pay off debt, and reach financial milestones without compromising their well-being or standard of living. Establishing reasonable financial objectives within the budget helps firms grow and be profitable, promoting long-term success as opposed to temporary benefits that might not be sustainable. Individuals and organizations can develop a budget that is inspiring, meaningful, and long-lasting by establishing attainable financial goals.

Keeping a healthy budget requires keeping track of spending. People and organizations can learn more about their financial habits, spot areas of overspending, and make necessary modifications to stay on track by routinely tracking their expenditures. Spreadsheets, budgeting applications, and even manual tracking techniques are some of the tools available for tracking spending. These tools assist with recording transactions, classifying expenses, and comparing actual spending to budgeted amounts. Because it gives a clear picture of where money is going and whether spending is in line with financial objectives, tracking expenses also promotes accountability. By keeping track of their spending, people can identify areas where they could be overpaying, like entertainment or eating out, and make deliberate changes. Keeping track of expenses is essential for organizations to manage operating costs, allocate resources as efficiently as possible, and make sure the budget aligns with strategic goals. In addition to keeping finances under control, tracking expenses is a great way to gather information that might aid with future budgeting. People and organizations can better understand their financial trends and work toward a more sustainable budget by regularly documenting their expenses.

An emphasis on long-term planning is also necessary to create a sustainable budget. Long-term planning entails establishing objectives and plans that promote financial security over the course of a lifetime, whereas short-term budgeting concentrates on controlling monthly income and expenses. This covers retirement preparation, key financial milestones, and major expenses like home ownership or school finance. While managing daily expenses, long-term planning within a budget guarantees that people are continuously working toward financial stability and independence. For instance, setting aside a small amount of money each month for retirement savings lays the groundwork for future financial stability. Financial planning and long-term budgeting help firms achieve capital investments, expansion plans, and other strategic objectives that need significant financial resources. Individuals and organizations can establish a strategy for long-term financial stability and make sure they are ready for upcoming opportunities and requirements by including long-term planning in their budget.

Beyond only ensuring financial stability, a sustainable budget offers several advantages, such as lowered stress levels, boosted self-esteem, and a greater sense of financial control. Many people experience financial stress, which can result in anxiety, strained relationships, and a decline in well-being. By providing a clear financial management plan, a sustainable budget helps people make educated decisions and steer clear of financial surprises, which helps to reduce some of this stress. Through enhancing financial resilience, a sustainable budget promotes a healthy connection with money by making people feel more prepared and safe. A sustainable budget lowers the risks that come with financial uncertainty for businesses, promoting a steady operating climate that fosters innovation and growth. A sustainable budget has psychological advantages that enhance general well-being by giving people and organizations the confidence to accomplish their objectives and deal with financial difficulties. A sustainable budget is the cornerstone of a more balanced, health-conscious approach to money and financial decision-making, not merely a financial tool.

To sum up, developing a sustainable budget is a thorough and continuous process that calls for knowledge of income, control of spending, setting realistic goals, prioritizing savings, lowering debt, and flexibility. It is an effective instrument for financial planning and analysis that gives people and organizations the flexibility, discipline, and structure they need to attain long-term financial stability. By encouraging financial resilience, a sustainable budget empowers people to face life's uncertainties with assurance and stability. A sustainable budget helps firms expand, be profitable, and stay stable by making sure that funds are used wisely to meet strategic goals. Individuals and organizations can build a foundation for long-term financial success by making budgeting a regular and flexible activity that helps them match their finances with their values, objectives, and long-term goals.

Adjusting the Budget for Changing Needs

For both individuals and businesses to maintain financial stability, achieve new objectives, and deal with unforeseen occurrences, it is imperative that the budget be adjusted for changing demands in financial planning and analysis. This process entails reviewing and modifying a financial plan in response to changing objectives, changes in the economy, or unforeseen circumstances that affect earnings, outlays, and overall financial well-being. Because financial conditions are rarely static and instead change in response to a range of internal and external events, such as changes in income, economic trends, new company endeavors, and changes in personal or organizational goals, budget adjustments are essential. In order to maintain financial health and distribute resources where they are most needed, effective financial planning recognizes the necessity of budgetary flexibility.

The foundation of financial planning and analysis is budgeting, which establishes a framework for investment, savings, and spending plans. A budget gives people a structure for controlling their daily spending, long-term financial objectives, and savings targets. Budgeting is more difficult for businesses since it must be in line with both operational and strategic goals. The budget serves as a financial road map in both situations, providing details on how funds will be distributed to achieve predetermined objectives. The presumptions made at the beginning of a budgetary cycle, however, are frequently vulnerable to modification. A hallmark of good financial management and a crucial component of maintaining alignment with financial goals is the capacity to evaluate and modify a budget in response to these developments.

Variability in revenue is one of the primary causes of budget modifications. Individuals' income may fluctuate as a result of things like employment changes, pay increases, or work schedule cutbacks. To make sure that financial objectives are still reachable within the new income limits, these changes call for a reevaluation of priorities and spending. Similar to this, companies' revenue varies according to competitive dynamics, market demand, and other economic factors. To preserve vital operations and long-term viability, it is critical to determine which discretionary expenses can be reduced or delayed as income declines. On the other hand, a rise in revenue can make it possible to pursue more ambitious objectives, such as raising investments, improving product offerings, or growing savings. Businesses and individuals can maximize their resources, prevent overspending, and get ready for any future variations by modifying their budgets to account for these changes.

The growing cost of living is another important aspect affecting budgetary changes. In order to preserve financial equilibrium, frequent adjustments are required due to inflationary pressures, including rising rent, food, healthcare, and educational expenses. Rising costs can put a burden on people's finances, necessitating either an increase in income-generating activities or a decrease in non-essential spending. Since more money is needed to cover basic expenses, rising living expenses may also have an effect on long-term savings and investment objectives in the context of financial planning and analysis. As the price of goods and services increases, businesses have comparable difficulties. They must constantly assess their budgets to find ways to increase pricing or boost efficiency without sacrificing competition if they want to stay profitable. To make sure that financial goals are still achievable in spite of the declining purchasing power, budgets must be modified in response to these inflationary pressures.

Unexpected events frequently necessitate budget adjustments in addition to changes in income and expenses. Financial stability can be significantly impacted by unforeseen events like medical crises, natural disasters, or economic downturns. The significance of having an emergency fund as part of financial planning is highlighted by the fact that unexpected medical expenses can put a burden on even a well-planned budget for individuals. In order to maintain operations, organizations may need to reallocate capital in response to unforeseen disruptions, such as supply chain problems or regulatory changes. A flexible budget that permits quick resource reallocation becomes crucial in these situations.

Individuals and organizations can handle unforeseen obstacles with little interference to their financial objectives by setting up contingency funds and periodically reviewing budgetary assumptions.

As corporate or personal objectives change, budget modifications are also required. Life events like marriage, having kids, or buying a house can drastically change financial priorities and necessitate a change in planning when it comes to personal finances. Starting a family, for example, usually results in higher living expenses; thus, budget allocations must be reviewed to make sure there are enough funds set aside for future needs, daycare, and schooling. Similar shifts in priority occur when organizations develop and mature. Fund reallocation is frequently necessary for new strategic goals like market expansion or R&D investments. By modifying the budget to account for these changing objectives, resources are allocated to projects that support the most recent aims, increasing the chances of success.

The act of modifying budgets to account for evolving needs is another area in which technology is revolutionary. The introduction of digital tools that enable real-time monitoring, forecasting, and scenario analysis has brought about a substantial evolution in financial planning and analysis. Financial dashboards and budgeting software allow both people and companies to keep a careful eye on their income and expenses, spot trends, and make necessary adjustments quickly. For example, people can use budgeting applications to receive real-time warnings about their spending habits, which helps them stick to their spending limitations or make changes before they go overboard. Financial modeling tools enable businesses to forecast how certain situations, such as lower income or higher capital expenditures, will affect the entire budget. Budget changes become more precise, timely, and in line with the evolving financial landscape when technology is used.

Although it's crucial to modify a budget to accommodate evolving needs, doing so calls for careful planning and prioritizing. Finding areas where small changes might meet the most urgent requirements without sacrificing long-term objectives is the aim; not all changes in financial conditions call for a total revision of the budget. For instance, cutting expenditures in other areas might be an option if expenses in one category routinely surpass projected amounts. Setting priorities guarantees that money is directed to areas that have the biggest influence on overall financial well-being, which is especially crucial when financial resources are scarce. In terms of personal economics, this could entail delaying discretionary expenditure in favor of critical costs like housing, food, and medical care. Setting priorities in the company may entail cutting back on non-essential projects while concentrating on ventures that will generate income or investments with a high rate of return.

Particularly inside organizations, cooperation, and communication are essential components of the budget adjustment process. The finance department rarely handles effective budgeting alone; assistance from other departments is needed to make sure the budget is in line with the organization's operational requirements and strategic goals. Frequent stakeholder communication makes it easier to spot any new requirements or possible financial limitations before they become issues. For example, a marketing department may anticipate that a new campaign will result in higher advertising costs, necessitating the involvement of finance to make the required budgetary adjustments. Organizations can make better-informed budget modifications that take into account the objectives and demands of every department by encouraging open communication. Regular evaluations and reassessments are essential to sound financial planning and analysis. Frequent budget reviews offer a chance to assess financial performance, contrast actual spending with planned spending, and pinpoint areas that could require revisions. Individuals can take corrective action before the conclusion of the budgeting cycle by identifying trends of overspending or underspending through a monthly or quarterly budget review. In accordance with the cycles of financial reporting, businesses often perform budget reviews on a quarterly basis. The finance team examines differences between expected and actual performance during these reviews, looks for possible inefficiencies, and modifies the budget to take into account the most recent financial information. Maintaining a proactive approach to financial management requires these frequent evaluations because they enable people and organizations to remain adaptable to shifting demands and conditions.

Many people and organizations employ a rolling budget, which continuously modifies financial estimates based on the most recent data available, in addition to regular evaluations. Rolling budgets offer flexibility by revising budget statistics often, usually on a monthly or quarterly basis, in contrast to static budgets that are set for a defined period. This method works especially well in dynamic settings where the state of the economy fluctuates regularly. A rolling budget, for instance, may be advantageous for companies operating in fast-paced sectors like technology or retail, as it may adapt to sudden changes in input costs or demand. Similarly, because rolling budgets allow for adjustments based on actual earnings rather than fixed estimates, they may be more appropriate for people with fluctuating incomes, such as commission-based workers or freelancers. Individuals and organizations can maintain flexibility in their financial planning and more easily adjust to evolving demands by implementing a rolling budget.

In the end, having a flexible and adaptable attitude is necessary to modify a budget to accommodate shifting needs. Financial planning is a continuous process that changes as new facts and situations arise rather than being a one-time event. Developing a proactive attitude to budgeting, where changes are seen as an essential component of financial management rather than an admission of failure, is advantageous for both individuals and companies. Because every budget modification offers a chance to enhance financial strategies, use resources optimally, and fortify overall financial resilience, this mindset promotes continual progress. Despite the uncertainty of the financial landscape, people and organizations can better handle financial obstacles and stay on course to accomplish their goals by embracing flexibility.

In summary, a crucial procedure in financial planning and analysis is modifying a budget to account for evolving needs. Through this process, people and organizations can efficiently adapt to changes in income, the cost of living, unanticipated circumstances, changing objectives, and technological breakthroughs. Budget modifications that are in line with present requirements and strategic goals are made possible by regular evaluations, prioritization, and open communication. The ability to proactively modify budgets when financial conditions change guarantees that resources are distributed effectively, financial stability is preserved, and long-term objectives are still reachable. In order to successfully traverse the complexity of the financial world, financial planning is a dynamic process that calls for ongoing monitoring, analysis, and change.

CHAPTER IV

Saving and Investing

The Role of Saving in Financial Planning

Savings is essential to financial planning and analysis because it provides a solid foundation for financial growth and stability for people, families, and businesses. Fundamentally, saving is the process of reserving a portion of earnings for future use. It acts as a safety net against unanticipated costs, a way to reach financial objectives, and a vital part in gradually accumulating wealth. Saving is a strategic choice that requires a thorough evaluation of one's income, expenses, and long-term goals in the framework of financial planning and analysis. By saving consistently, people and organizations build the foundation for a more secure financial future by being better prepared to handle both anticipated and unforeseen financial demands.

Creating a financial safety net is one of the main purposes of saving in financial planning. From unforeseen repairs or natural catastrophes to medical problems and job loss, life is full of unknowns. Having a specific savings fund can help lessen the financial effects of these occurrences. An emergency fund is a type of savings that acts as a buffer in personal finance, enabling people and families to pay for unforeseen costs without taking on debt. Usually, this emergency fund is kept in a liquid account that is accessible when needed, like a savings account. Although this amount might vary based on individual circumstances, such as employment stability and personal risk tolerance, it is generally advised to save three to six months' worth of living expenses in an emergency fund. People who have a healthy emergency savings account are less likely to face financial difficulties when things become tough, protecting their financial stability and allowing them to concentrate on long-term objectives.

Savings has a similar function for organizations and frequently manifest as cash reserves or retained earnings. Businesses with sufficient cash reserves are better equipped to handle unforeseen operating costs, take advantage of new possibilities, and weather economic downturns without endangering their financial stability. Businesses with substantial cash reserves, for instance, can continue to operate, pay their employees, and possibly even engage in expansion plans during a recession, whilst others would find it difficult to make it through. Cash reserves can also give businesses the adaptability they need to execute smart purchases or adjust to changes in the market. Savings thus turn into a crucial part of risk management, allowing businesses to stay financially stable despite opportunities and problems.

Savings not only act as a financial safety net but also make it possible to reach certain financial objectives. These objectives can be anything from buying a house or paying for college to organizing a wedding or a dream getaway. Saving promotes a sense of financial security and independence by enabling people to work toward their goals without taking on debt. Savings and goal-setting are frequently combined in financial planning because well-defined financial objectives offer guidance and inspiration. People can go steadily toward their objectives by methodically saving aside money, which will guarantee that they have enough cash on hand for significant investments or life purchases. Savings not only make it easier to accomplish goals, but they also foster a disciplined approach to money management and strengthen sound financial practices that can result in long-term financial success.

Saving becomes even more important when it comes to retirement planning. For many people, personal savings are now their only source of retirement income due to rising life expectancies and the decline in traditional pension schemes. In order to benefit from compound interest, which earns interest on both the original principal and the accrued interest, financial advisors frequently stress the significance of beginning retirement savings as early as feasible. People who save regularly over time can accumulate a sizeable retirement fund that will give them the money they need to continue living the way they want to in retirement. A number of retirement accounts, including IRAs, Roth IRAs, and 401(k)s, provide tax benefits that encourage retirement savings even more. Retirement savings are a crucial part of financial planning and analysis since contributions to these accounts not only help people prepare for the future but also may result in tax savings now.

Savings are also essential for firms to finance expansion plans and long-term projects. Businesses can explore new endeavors, enter new markets, or create new products without exclusively depending on outside funding if they have enough savings, which are frequently in the form of retained earnings or investment capital. Self-funding expansion plans have several benefits, including lowering reliance on debt financing and lowering the risk of dilution for current shareholders. Additionally, because they exhibit consistency and financial prudence, companies with robust internal funding sources are frequently seen more favorably by credit rating agencies and investors. Savings thus promote strategic growth and operational resilience, allowing businesses to pursue chances for innovation and expansion while establishing a sound financial base.

Savings are essential to building wealth in addition to helping achieve particular objectives. Individuals and organizations can increase their savings over time and create wealth that can be passed down to future generations or used to pay for future needs by consistently laying aside money and making prudent investments. People can become financially independent by building wealth through investing and saving, which means they won't require active income to cover their expenses. People may choose their careers and lifestyles without worrying about money thanks to this independence, which gives them a sense of security and freedom. A family's acquired wealth can also be a legacy, giving future generations the means to follow their dreams of entrepreneurship, education, or other endeavors. In this situation, saving is a way to build long-term financial security and opportunity rather than just a financial habit.

In addition to conserving money, effective financial planning calls for a strategic study of how much to save, where to put savings, and how to maximize returns. Saving without a plan may result in resources being misallocated or opportunities being lost. To figure out how much to save in relation to income and expenses, financial analysis methods like forecasting, budgeting, and cash flow analysis are crucial. People might find areas where they might be able to boost their savings by examining their financial circumstances, whether it is by maximizing debt payments, reducing discretionary expenditure, or raising income. To evaluate cash flow and decide how much of their revenue can be set aside for reserves or reinvested in the company, organizations employ comparable analytical tools. With the help of these assessments, people and organizations may make well-informed saving choices that complement their larger financial plans.

Savings plays a part in both financial and investment planning. Savings is the first step toward financial stability, but investing gives you the chance to increase your savings over time. Both saving and investing are common components of a solid financial plan, with investments offering the possibility of larger returns and saves acting as a steady, low-risk reserve. Since it provides the funds required to seize investment possibilities, saving is the first step in this process. For instance, a person may start investing in stocks, bonds, or real estate to increase their wealth after they have established an emergency fund and put money aside for immediate necessities. In a similar vein, businesses frequently spend a portion of their cash reserves in investment portfolios in an effort to produce returns that support their overall financial well-being. Financial planning becomes a comprehensive approach that strikes a balance between stability and growth when saving and investing are combined.

Financial well-being is significantly impacted psychologically by saving as well. According to research, those who save regularly report feeling less stressed about money and more confident about their financial future. The assurance that a financial buffer is in place helps ease worry related to unforeseen costs or changes in income. In the current economic environment, when job security and income stability can be unpredictable, this psychological benefit is especially crucial. Because it shows a dedication to long-term stability and financial prudence, having a healthy savings fund can also increase trust among stakeholders, including as management, employees, and investors. Thus, saving promotes a sense of security and resilience that supports both individual and organizational growth, in addition to improving financial health and general well-being.

Additionally, saving fosters a long-term outlook in financial analysis and planning. Savings necessitates patience, discipline, and a dedication to long-term objectives— qualities that are critical for effective money management. By regularly putting money aside, people and organizations cultivate a mindset that values financial sustainability by learning to put long-term gains ahead of short-term satisfaction. This long-term outlook is essential for successful financial planning because it pushes people and organizations to think beyond immediate profits and take the bigger picture into account when making financial decisions. When saving for retirement, for instance, people must consider decades into the future and imagine a time when they will need their collected wealth to sustain their standard of living. In a similar vein, companies that put saving first are better positioned to accomplish their strategic goals because they may devote funds to initiatives that might not pay off for years. Savings supports the goal of long-term financial success by encouraging a forward-thinking mindset, which improves the efficacy of financial planning and analysis.

The importance of saving in financial planning is more than ever in the quickly evolving economic climate of today. Market volatility, inflation, and economic uncertainty highlight the necessity of having a safety net to guard against unforeseen difficulties. Savings gives people a way to adjust to changes in the economy, including growing expenses or shifts in income. Savings gives businesses the adaptability they need to handle operational risks, take advantage of new opportunities, and navigate market swings. In this way, saving is a proactive tactic that improves financial agility rather than just a protective one. Strong savings funds help people and organizations be resilient and capable of reaching their financial goals by enabling them to react more effectively to shifting economic situations.

To sum up, saving is a fundamental component of financial planning and analysis, fulfilling a number of vital roles that support long-term success, goal attainment, financial stability, and asset growth. It gives people and organizations a financial safety net so they may confidently face uncertainty. The pursuit of particular financial objectives, such as home ownership, retirement funding, or business expansion, is also supported by saving. Additionally, saving is crucial for developing wealth, which paves the way for legacy-building and financial independence. Individuals and organizations can maximize their resources and make well-informed decisions that support their long-term goals by conducting financial analyses and allocating savings strategically. Psychologically, saving creates a long-term perspective that improves the efficacy of financial planning, eases financial stress, and promotes peace of mind. The significance of saving in financial planning and analysis is unwavering despite the ongoing changes in the economy, highlighting its function as a vital element of resilience and financial health.

Investment Fundamentals

Investment fundamentals give people and organizations the tools they need to accomplish growth, wealth accumulation, and long-term financial security. They are a key component of financial planning and analysis. Fundamentally, investing is the process of putting resources—typically cash—into assets with the hope of earning a return later on. Financial planning requires effective investment methods in order for investors to accomplish their short- and long-term financial objectives, accumulate wealth, and plan for future expenses. Understanding different investment kinds, risk and return concepts, diversification, and the compounding effects of time are all necessary for this process. Investment fundamentals aid in decision-making by ensuring that people and organizations make well-informed decisions that fit their time horizon, risk tolerance, and financial goals.

Knowing the various asset classes and how they fit into a financial strategy is one of the most important parts of investing. In general, there are several types of investment assets, each having unique traits and risk profiles, including stocks, bonds, real estate, and cash equivalents. Although stocks, also known as equities, provide the possibility of large gains and symbolize ownership in a company, they are also highly volatile in the market. Bonds, on the other hand, are fixed-income securities that are appealing to investors looking for a lower-risk option since they usually offer more consistent, predictable returns. Investing in real estate entails buying a property with the hope of eventually seeing capital growth or rental revenue. Certificates of deposit (CDs) and savings accounts are examples of cash equivalents. They are extremely liquid investments with low risk and modest returns. Investors can create a diversified portfolio that strikes a balance between stability and growth potential by knowing the traits of each asset class and selecting a combination of investments that suit their risk tolerance and financial objectives.

Two key ideas in investing are risk and return, which act as a framework for assessing possible investments. Every investment has a certain amount of risk, or the potential to lose money or make less than expected. In general, increased risk is linked to higher returns, and lower risk is typically linked to lower returns. In financial planning and analysis, this relationship is essential because it enables investors to determine whether the possible return on investment outweighs the risk involved. For instance, stocks have a high potential return but are prone to market volatility, which means that their value can change dramatically over brief periods of time. Even though they are generally safer, bonds might yield lesser returns, especially when interest rates are low. The capacity to determine one's risk tolerance or the amount of risk an investor is willing and able to endure, is a crucial component of investment fundamentals. Given that they have more time to recoup from any losses, younger investors with longer time horizons might be more likely to invest in riskier assets like equities. On the other hand, people who are getting close to retirement might place more importance on capital preservation and choose safer assets to safeguard their funds. Investors can make decisions that suit their own financial objectives and situation by comprehending and weighing risk and return.

Another crucial idea in investing is diversification, which reduces risk by distributing funds over several assets, sectors, and regions. The negative performance of any one investment has less of an effect on total returns when the portfolio is well-diversified. For instance, if the technology sector collapses, an investor who only invests in technology equities may suffer large losses. Nonetheless, the investor can lessen their exposure to any one source of risk by spreading their money over a variety of stocks, bonds, real estate, and foreign assets. A diversified portfolio can yield more consistent returns in a range of market scenarios because diversification works on the premise that not all assets will perform well at the same time. Diversification is a key component of financial planning and analysis because it helps investors manage risk and obtain more consistent outcomes without compromising their ability to develop. Investors can minimize the possibility of large losses while building a portfolio that fits their financial objectives and risk tolerance by distributing their assets across a variety of asset classes and industries.

Another important factor in investment fundamentals is time horizon, which is the amount of time an investor intends to hold an investment before having to access the money. A key consideration when choosing an investment plan is the time horizon, which affects the kinds of assets that make up a portfolio. Investors who have long-term objectives, like retirement, can decide to put their money into growth-oriented assets, like equities, which have the potential to yield larger returns over time. The more time you have to weather market turbulence and take advantage of compounding returns—where profits create more profits—the longer your investment horizon. On the other hand, investors may favor lower-risk assets, such as bonds or cash equivalents, which offer more stability and liquidity, for short-term objectives. Time horizon is given a lot of weight in financial planning and analysis because it helps investors make choices that support their objectives and priorities while guaranteeing that money will be available when needed. Individuals and organizations can optimize their portfolios to fulfill specific objectives within the appropriate timeframe by taking the time horizon into account when planning their investments.

A significant idea in investing is compounding, which enables investors to profit from both their initial investment and their cumulative gains. Compounding has the potential to greatly raise an investment's value over time, particularly when reinvested profits provide further gains. When an investor reinvests interest earned on a bond, for instance, their investment will increase faster than if they just received the money without doing anything with it. Early savers and investors profit from compounding since it has an exponentially growing effect over time. Compounding can be more advantageous for an individual with a longer investing horizon. When it comes to retirement planning, this idea is especially crucial because modest, regular payments over a long period of time can add up to significant amounts by the time of retirement. The significance of compounding as a strategy for wealth building is frequently emphasized in financial planning and analysis, which encourages people to begin investing as soon as possible in order to optimize their returns over time. An investor's capacity to reach their financial objectives can be greatly improved by comprehending and utilizing the force of compounding, which enables money to increase more quickly.

A key component of investment strategy is asset allocation, which is the process of dividing up investments among several asset classes in order to attain the appropriate ratio of return to risk. An investor's objectives, risk tolerance, and time horizon are taken into consideration when allocating assets in financial planning and analysis, resulting in a portfolio that is specifically matched to their requirements. An older investor approaching retirement would favor a combination of bonds and cash equivalents for stability, whereas a younger individual with a high-risk tolerance might have a portfolio that is heavily weighted in equities. Asset allocation is dynamic and needs to be modified on a regular basis in response to shifts in the investor's objectives, financial status, and market conditions. A crucial component of investment management is rebalancing a portfolio, which involves modifying the asset allocation to preserve the appropriate degree of risk and guaranteeing that the portfolio stays in line with the investor's goals. Asset allocation is emphasized in financial planning and analysis as a crucial instrument for risk management, return enhancement, and portfolio performance optimization. Investors can build a diversified portfolio that supports their financial objectives and lowers the risk of significant losses by choosing the appropriate mix of assets.

Planning for investments also requires an understanding of market cycles since asset prices are impacted by the expansion and contraction of markets. While bear markets, which are characterized by declining prices, can result in large losses for investors, bull markets, which are characterized by rising prices, frequently offer great returns. Knowing market cycles enables investors to make well-informed choices about whether to purchase, hold, or sell assets, maximizing profits and reducing losses. Financial planning and analysis can assist investors in identifying patterns and trends that may indicate the stage of a market cycle, even though it is impossible to predict market movements with absolute precision. While some investors may employ timing tactics to profit from market cycles, others may choose to buy and hold their investments regardless of market volatility. Investors can increase their chances of long-term financial success by making better decisions about whether to enter or exit the market by having a better understanding of market cycles and how they affect asset prices.

Understanding economic indicators and how they affect asset performance is another aspect of investment fundamentals. In addition to influencing the performance of different asset classes, economic indicators like GDP growth, inflation, unemployment rates, and interest rates offer insights into the state of the economy as a whole. Rising interest rates, for example, can have a negative effect on bond values since they reduce the appeal of older bonds by offering higher returns. Conversely, inflation reduces purchasing power and has an impact on actual investment results. Investors can make well-informed decisions on how to modify their portfolios to reflect shifting economic conditions by examining economic data. In order to help investors predict how various assets would perform under various economic situations, financial planning and analysis rely on economic indicators to guide investment decisions. Investors should make proactive portfolio modifications and make sure their assets are positioned to perform effectively in shifting economic environments by being aware of how economic trends affect investing.

Since taxes have the potential to drastically lower investment returns, tax efficiency is yet another crucial component of investment fundamentals. Maximizing after-tax returns requires an awareness of the many tax treatment options available for different investment types. For instance, compared to short-term gains, capital gains on assets held for more than a year are usually taxed at a lower rate. Furthermore, investments can grow tax-deferred or even tax-free in tax-advantaged accounts like IRAs, 401(k)s, and Health Savings Accounts (HSAs), offering significant chances for tax-efficient investing. In order to help investors choose the most tax-efficient investments for their portfolios, financial planning and analysis place a strong emphasis on tax efficiency as a means of increasing profits. Tax-efficient investing is a crucial part of good financial planning because it allows investors to keep more of their earnings, which improves their ability to meet their financial objectives. By taking tax implications into account, investors can make decisions that reduce their tax liability and allow more of their returns to contribute to wealth accumulation.

A growing area of study within investment basics is behavioral finance, which examines how psychological aspects affect investment choices. Overconfidence, loss aversion, and herd mentality are examples of behavioral biases that can cause investors to make illogical decisions that have a detrimental effect on their portfolios. For example, loss aversion might drive an investor to avoid required risks, reducing their potential profits, while overconfidence can cause them to take unnecessary risks. Developing a disciplined investment plan requires an understanding of these behavioral biases because it empowers investors to make logical decisions based on analysis rather than emotion. Behavioral finance insights are frequently included in financial planning and analysis, assisting investors in identifying and reducing the impact of biases on their choices. Individuals and organizations can make more consistent, unbiased decisions that fit their risk tolerance and financial objectives by continuing to take a disciplined approach to investing.

In conclusion, the information and resources required to create a portfolio that supports long-term financial goals are provided by investing fundamentals, which are essential to financial planning and analysis. Investors can make well-informed decisions that support their objectives by having a solid understanding of asset types, risk and return, diversification, time horizon, and the power of compounding. Investment strategy is further improved by asset allocation, market cycle awareness, economic indicator analysis, tax efficiency, and behavioral finance, which enables investors to manage risk and maximize returns. Individuals and organizations can develop a strong investment strategy that promotes resilience, stability, and financial growth in a continuously changing economic environment by putting these concepts into practice. These foundational principles enable investors to successfully negotiate the intricacies of the financial markets, setting them up for long-term financial success.

Diversifying Investments for Stability

In financial planning and analysis, diversifying investments is one of the best ways to attain financial stability since it provides a buffer against volatility and a route to long-term growth. Fundamentally, diversification is the process of distributing assets throughout several asset classes, industries, and geographical areas in order to lower exposure to the risk involved with any one asset. The portfolio is less susceptible to changes in certain markets or individual investments when its assets are diversified. Diversification is based on the notion that different assets will respond differently to changes in the market or economy; therefore, when certain assets perform poorly, others may hold steady or even increase in value. By attempting to strike a balance between risk and return, diversification gives investors the stability they need to pursue their financial objectives, something that is not possible when they only invest in one or two asset classes. Strategic planning, in-depth knowledge of asset classes, and a dedication to routinely rebalancing and modifying a portfolio as markets and personal financial objectives change are all necessary for effective diversification.

Diversification reduces unsystematic risk, or the risk associated with individual investments, which is one of the main reasons it is so successful in fostering stability. Unsystematic risk encompasses elements unique to a given business or sector, like leadership changes, customer preferences, or regulatory advancements that could affect a company's performance. Investors might lessen their exposure to these isolated risks by distributing their money over several industries and businesses. For example, an investor's portfolio may sustain large losses if it is highly concentrated in technology companies and the industry declines as a result of new regulatory restrictions. However, the negative effects of the technological slump would be mitigated by the perhaps stable or positive performance in other sectors if that portfolio also included investments in utilities, real estate, and healthcare. By lowering dependence on any one investment, diversification acts as a safeguard against unanticipated problems that can have a detrimental impact on certain assets.

Choosing assets from a variety of classes, including stocks, bonds, real estate, and commodities, is another aspect of diversification that goes beyond simply distributing investments across several industries. Every asset type has unique traits and behaves differently in different economic environments. For example, stocks have the potential to yield larger profits, but they are typically more volatile, particularly in the short term. Conversely, bonds are regarded as lower-risk investments that offer a set income and are less vulnerable to daily changes in the market. While commodities like gold and oil can give stability during uncertain economic times or periods of inflationary pressure, real estate offers physical assets and can serve as a hedge against inflation. Investors can balance prospective growth with the stability of lower-risk investments by combining various asset types to construct a portfolio that capitalizes on each one's advantages. For instance, bonds may hold steady or even rise in value during a stock market collapse as investors look for safer alternatives, maintaining the overall value of a diversified portfolio.

By distributing investments throughout several nations and areas, geographic diversity further improves an investment portfolio's stability. Because market dynamics, political stability, and economic conditions can differ greatly throughout regions, investments made in different places might not be impacted by the same occurrences. Investors can lessen their exposure to the economic hazards of a particular nation or region by diversifying globally. For instance, if the U.S. economy goes into a recession, an investor who only owns U.S. stocks might lose money. However, since other economies may perform differently, the portfolio may be less impacted overall if they also hold investments in European or emerging market assets. Geographic diversity strikes a balance that fosters resilience and stability in a range of market scenarios by enabling investors to take advantage of growth prospects in emerging nations while also enjoying the stability of more developed economies. Additionally, currency exchange rates can contribute to regional diversification since shifts in exchange rates can impact the returns on foreign investments, which increases the advantage of diversification.

Another crucial element of a sound investing plan is diversification within asset classes. For instance, an investor may diversify among many industries, like technology, healthcare, finance, consumer goods, and energy, within the stock asset class. Diversification by sector lessens the impact of unfavorable occurrences that could impact a certain industry. Similar to this, diversification within bonds can be accomplished by purchasing bonds from different issuers, corporations, and municipalities, as well as by investing in bonds with different maturity dates and credit ratings. This strategy guards against inflationary pressures, credit concerns, and interest rate fluctuations. Investments in residential, commercial, and industrial real estate as well as real estate investment trusts (REITs), which provide access to real estate markets without requiring direct property ownership, are further options for diversification in the real estate industry. Investors can further lower the particular risks associated with any one investment type by diversifying within each asset class, which guarantees that the portfolio will stay steady even in the event that one section performs poorly.

The foundation of diversity is the idea of correlation. Investments with low or negative correlation typically perform differently in comparable market conditions. Correlation assesses how investments move in relation to one another. For instance, there is frequently little to no correlation between stocks and bonds, which means that when stock prices decline, bond prices may increase or stay the same. Because gains in one sector may counterbalance losses in another, investors can develop a balanced strategy that stabilizes returns by combining assets with low or negative correlations in their portfolio. Long-term stability depends on this balance since it evens out the highs and lows of the performance of individual assets, lowering the volatility of the entire portfolio. Correlation serves as a guide for creating a diverse portfolio in financial planning and analysis, which includes assets with various performance patterns. This strategy increases the possibility of long-term, consistent returns by ensuring that the portfolio is not unduly exposed to any one risk factor.

Since different investment kinds are better suited for different time frames, time horizon also plays a big part in a diversification strategy. Growth-oriented assets like equities, which have the potential for better returns over lengthy periods of time despite short-term volatility, maybe the focus of a portfolio for long-term objectives like retirement. To shield acquired wealth from future market downturns, the portfolio may change to contain a larger percentage of low-risk assets like bonds and cash equivalents as the time horizon gets shorter. This slow change called a glide path technique, improves stability as the investor gets closer to their objective by balancing the risk level of the portfolio with their financial requirements. Therefore, time-based diversification entails periodically rebalancing the portfolio to take into account the investor's evolving financial goals and circumstances. Time horizon considerations are crucial in financial planning and analysis because they help create a diversified portfolio that is stable and relevant throughout different phases of life and financial circumstances.

Maintaining a diverse portfolio that fits an investor's objectives and risk tolerance requires regular rebalancing. Market performance can cause the values of various investments in a portfolio to fluctuate over time, which can alter the asset allocation of the portfolio. For instance, equities may make up a bigger percentage of the portfolio than originally planned if they do very well, raising the risk level of the portfolio. Rebalancing entails modifying the portfolio by purchasing or disposing of assets in order to return them to their initial allocation. By ensuring that the portfolio stays in line with the investor's financial objectives and risk tolerance, this method gradually improves stability. By selling high-performing assets and reinvesting in undervalued ones, rebalancing enables investors to capitalize on market circumstances and increase returns while preserving the desired diversification. Regular rebalancing is essential to financial planning and analysis because it maintains the

CHAPTER V

Debt Management

Types of Debt and Their Impact
Debt is a crucial part of financial planning and analysis since it offers individuals, companies, and governments both opportunities and risks. An entity's capacity to satisfy future financial obligations, development potential, and financial stability are all significantly impacted by the kinds of debt it has and how it is managed. In its most basic definition, debt is borrowed funds that have to be paid back with interest. However, there are many other kinds of debt, each with unique features, conditions, and financial effects. In order to create strategies for managing responsibilities, maximizing cash flows, and reaching financial objectives while lowering risk, it is essential to have a thorough understanding of these many forms of debt. Every type of debt, from credit cards and consumer loans to government debt and corporate bonds, has certain benefits and disadvantages that should be considered in light of an organization's long-term goals and overall financial health. To make wise decisions and achieve balanced financial growth, one must have a solid awareness of the many forms of debt and how they affect financial planning.

One of the most common forms of debt that affect both people and households is consumer debt. Among other things, it covers credit cards, school loans, auto loans, and personal loans. Due to high interest rates and revolving credit lengths, credit card debt is very prevalent and can be among the most difficult to manage. Credit card debt enables users to carry a load from month to month, earning interest on the remaining balance, in contrast to installment loans. If not handled appropriately, this revolving nature might result in a debt cycle because interest builds up on the outstanding balance over time, raising the total amount due. An individual's credit score, which influences their ability to obtain favorable terms on future loans, can be adversely affected by high credit card debt. Since credit card debt is a costly liability that can impede chances for investment and saving, managing it is essential in financial planning. Financial planners frequently recommend paying off high-interest credit card debt as soon as possible in order to lessen its impact. They do this by reducing balances in a methodical manner utilizing techniques like the avalanche or snowball methods.

Personal loans, another type of consumer debt, are usually unsecured loans that can be used for a number of things, such as funding large purchases or consolidating existing debts. Personal loans can be easier to manage than credit card debt because they often have fixed interest rates and repayment terms. However, depending on the borrower's creditworthiness, interest rates may still be relatively high because they are frequently unsecured. Personal loans are occasionally regarded as a good choice in financial planning for combining several high-interest debts since they can make payments easier and possibly result in lower total interest expenses. But they also increase the borrower's overall debt load, which may have an impact on their debt-to-income ratio—a crucial metric that lenders evaluate to determine a borrower's capacity to take on more credit. A key component of financial analysis is the debt-to-income ratio, which shows the percentage of income devoted to debt repayment and affects a person's creditworthiness and financial flexibility.

Another major source of consumer debt is student loans, especially in areas where the cost of education is high. Both the government and private lenders may offer these loans, which are usually used to pay for higher education. When compared to private student loans, federal student loans frequently offer more flexible repayment choices, such as deferment and income-driven payments, along with lower interest rates. However, it might take decades to pay back student loan debt, which limits borrowers' capacity to invest, save, or make significant life decisions like purchasing a home. Since student loan debt is linked to an investment in human capital that may result in greater lifetime earnings, it is frequently seen as a type of "good debt" in financial planning. However, many graduates' heavy debt loads can put a strain on their finances, necessitating careful payment prioritizing and budgeting to prevent default. Strategic repayment planning is crucial since defaulting on student loans can have serious repercussions, such as salary garnishment and worse credit scores.

Another kind of consumer debt is auto loans, which are frequently backed by the car itself. Over the course of the loan, customers can make predictable monthly payments because auto loans usually have set interest rates and terms. Although they might still vary greatly depending on creditworthiness, interest rates for secured auto loans are often lower than those for unsecured personal loans. However, because automobiles lose value quickly, buyers can find themselves "underwater" on their loan—that is, owing more than the car's market value. Since auto loans enable customers to buy a critical asset without incurring a substantial upfront cost, they are typically regarded as a manageable type of debt in financial planning as long as they are kept within appropriate bounds. However, in order to prevent long-term debt on a declining asset, financial advisors frequently counsel their clients to strive for shorter loan periods and higher down payments.

One of the biggest and most prevalent forms of debt for both people and households is mortgage debt. Mortgages are backed by the actual property and are used to buy real estate. Because they are secured, mortgages often have extended repayment terms—typically 15 to 30 years—and offer comparatively low interest rates when compared to other forms of consumer lending. Since real estate can increase in value over time and raise a homeowner's net worth, mortgage debt is frequently regarded as a "good debt." Additionally, mortgage interest is frequently tax deductible, which is a financial advantage that can lower the loan's total cost. Mortgage debt is typically seen in financial planning as a means of accumulating wealth, especially when handled sensibly. High mortgage payments, however, might put a burden on a household's budget, especially if housing expenses are above the suggested monthly income %. Furthermore, if interest rates increase, adjustable-rate mortgages (ARMs) may become riskier due to increased monthly payments. To make sure the debt is in line with long-term financial objectives, financial analysis of mortgage debt usually entails assessing the loan terms, interest rate type, and refinancing possibility.

From consumer to corporate debt, businesses frequently utilize a variety of loans to fund capital projects, operations, and expansion. One popular kind of corporate debt is corporate bonds, which are issued by businesses to investors in return for funding. In corporate bonds, the principle is paid back to bondholders after a certain period of fixed interest payments. In general, corporate bonds are riskier than government bonds but less hazardous than stocks. The interest rates that are given are determined by the credit rating of the corporation. Since corporate bonds have no effect on shareholder equity, they can be a useful tool for businesses looking to borrow capital without reducing ownership, according to financial planning and research. High corporate debt, however, might raise financial risk, particularly if the company's profits aren't enough to pay interest. A company's capacity to borrow money at advantageous rates is influenced by the ratings that credit rating organizations provide after evaluating the risk of corporate debt. Although investors must take credit risk and default risk into account, corporate bonds offer them the chance to earn interest income.

Commercial loans, which businesses get from banks or other financial organizations, are another kind of corporate debt. These loans can be used for a number of things, such as expansion, equipment acquisitions, and operating capital. Depending on the company's credit rating, loan purpose, and ability to repay, commercial loans can be either secured or unsecured, with different terms and interest rates. Commercial loans are essential for short- to medium-term capital that supports a business's operations and expansion, according to financial research. However, a company's cash flow may be strained by an over-reliance on commercial loans, especially if interest rates are high or income is declining. When working with firms, financial planners frequently concentrate on optimizing debt structures to strike a balance between reasonable payback responsibilities and development potential.

Although they aren't necessarily considered debt, leases are another type of liability that businesses utilize to fund assets like real estate, cars, and equipment. While financing leases are more like installment loans in that ownership is transferred at the conclusion of the lease term, operating leases let businesses use assets without assuming ownership in exchange for a monthly payment. Leases are frequently seen in financial planning as an adaptable means of gaining access to assets without incurring large upfront expenses. Although accounting regulations have made it more and more necessary for businesses to record leases as liabilities on the balance sheet, leases are still considered an off-balance-sheet funding source for financial analysis. Companies looking to save money or avoid long-term debt may find leasing beneficial, but it must be carefully considered to make sure that the advantages of asset ownership are not outweighed by leasing expenses.

Another important issue is government debt, which has an impact on both domestic and international financial markets. To fund social programs, infrastructure development, and public projects, governments issue bonds. Because government bonds are guaranteed by the government's authority to impose taxes or print money, they are generally seen as low-risk investments. However, if the government has to reallocate resources to pay off debt, excessive government debt may result in greater taxes, inflation, and a reduction in public services. Government debt contributes to retirement and investment portfolios as a source of reliable, income-producing assets in financial planning. High amounts of government debt, however, might raise concerns in financial analysis, especially if they become unmanageable and could result in fiscal crises or a decline in public trust in the government's ability to pay its debts.

The debt-to-equity ratio, which calculates the percentage of debt in an entity's capital structure as opposed to equity, is one of the most important metrics in debt research. When a business or individual depends significantly on borrowed cash, a high debt-to-equity ratio may be a sign of financial leverage. Leverage can boost returns, but it also raises risk because fixed debt payments are required regardless of revenue or income levels. A balanced debt-to-equity ratio is essential for both loan availability and financial stability in financial planning. If cash flows are not enough to pay off debt, excessive leverage can restrict an entity's ability to take on more debt and result in financial difficulty.

Debt has an impact on cash flow, liquidity, and investment prospects, in addition to repayment responsibilities when it comes to financial planning and analysis. High debt levels can also limit financial flexibility, and debt payments lower disposable income, which limits the ability to save or invest. In financial planning, managing debt entails striking a balance between present demands and long-term aims to make sure that debt commitments don't get in the way of reaching financial goals. In order to lower the cost of capital, preserve financial flexibility, and foster long-term growth, firms must optimize their capital structure as part of debt management.

In conclusion, there are many different kinds of debt, each with unique ramifications, making it a complex part of financial planning and analysis. It is crucial to comprehend the traits and dangers of each sort of debt, whether managing government, business, or consumer debt. In order to keep debt levels sustainable and in line with long-term financial objectives, financial planning seeks to use debt as a tool for stability and growth. Entities may safeguard cash flow, improve financial stability, and set themselves up for future success by managing their debt well. In a world where debt is becoming more and more important in both personal and business finances, managing debt well is essential to building resilience and financial health.

Strategies for Reducing Debt

Debt reduction affects both personal financial well-being and overall economic stability, making it an essential part of financial planning and analysis. Strategies for reducing debt are intended to ease the strain of unpaid debts, enhance cash flow, and free up funds for investments, savings, and other financial objectives. If not properly handled, debt—whether it comes from governments, businesses, or individuals—can become a major limitation. Excessive debt makes it harder to attain long- term financial stability, strains finances and makes one more susceptible to economic downturns. Reducing debt is frequently a top priority for people in order to manage financial stress and make it possible to achieve future objectives like retirement savings or property. While governments must reduce debt to prevent fiscal crises and foster economic growth, firms can benefit from debt management by optimizing capital structure and maintaining financial flexibility. A strategic strategy is necessary for effective debt reduction, integrating budgeting, prioritizing debts, disciplined repayment schedules, and knowledge of the variables that contribute to debt accumulation.

Making a strict and realistic budget is a basic debt reduction method. By giving people or organizations a clear picture of their income and expenses, budgeting enables them to spot areas where expenses can be cut, or resources can be shifted toward debt repayment. A well-planned budget prioritizes necessary spending and sets aside extra money for high-interest debt repayment, which, over time, can drastically lower the total amount due. This sometimes entails setting up a monthly budget for individuals who place a higher priority on housing, food, transportation, and other essentials while reducing discretionary spending until debt levels are under control. However, in order to pay off debt, organizations could reallocate cash from less important operational areas. Budgeting is essential to financial planning and analysis because it guarantees that resources are distributed efficiently, laying the groundwork for other debt reduction tactics.

The "avalanche" and "snowball" methods, which provide systematic procedures for paying off various loans, are also effective debt reduction strategies. Regardless of interest rate, the snowball method entails paying off debts in order of highest to lowest balance. By paying off fewer loans first, this strategy gives borrowers a sense of immediate success, which may motivate them to stick to their repayment schedules. On the other hand, regardless of balance, the avalanche strategy prioritizes paying off the loans with the greatest interest rates first. The avalanche strategy can save more money over time by lowering the overall amount of interest paid, even if it could take longer to notice returns at first. The choice between the avalanche and snowball approaches in financial planning is based on interest rates, debt levels, and personal preferences. Both approaches offer a methodical approach to debt management, lessening the total load and establishing a planned route to financial independence.

Another common method for reducing debt is debt consolidation, particularly for people who have several high-interest bills. Combining several debts into one loan—ideally with a lower interest rate and more manageable terms of repayment—is known as debt consolidation. Because borrowers only have to concentrate on one monthly payment, this approach can streamline repayment and lower the chance of default or missed payments. Personal loans, home equity loans, and balance transfer credit cards are the most typical ways to obtain consolidation loans; each has certain conditions and qualifying requirements. For debtors who are eligible for advantageous conditions, debt consolidation is frequently advised in financial planning since it can lower monthly payments and overall interest expenses, improving the efficiency of debt repayment. Debt consolidation should be used carefully, though, as it restructures debt rather than removes it, and borrowers must refrain from taking on new debt while repaying the consolidation loan.

Another debt reduction tactic for people with high-interest credit card debt is to move balances to a card with a low or zero percent introductory interest rate. For a short time, usually six to eighteen months, borrowers can move their old balances to a new card with no interest or a very low interest rate, thanks to promotional balance transfer rates offered by many credit card issuers. Borrowers can concentrate on reducing the principal amount during this promotional time without paying extra interest, thus speeding up the debt reduction process. However, there are frequent costs associated with balance transfers, and the interest rate may return to a significantly higher level if the balance is not paid off before the conclusion of the promotional term. Balance transfers are strategically employed in financial planning to lower interest costs and speed up repayment; however, in order to optimize savings, borrowers must have a strategy in place to pay off the remaining amount during the promotional period.

Another successful debt reduction tactic is negotiating with creditors, especially for people or companies who are struggling financially. If they think it will increase the possibility of payback, many creditors are ready to drop interest rates, negotiate payment plans, or even accept a smaller payoff amount. By arranging a lump sum payment that is less than the entire amount owed, debt settlement enables borrowers to pay off debt at a reduced rate. However, any forgiven debt can be seen as taxable income, and debt settlement can have a negative effect on credit scores. Credit counseling services can help consumers with high debt levels negotiate with creditors and create affordable repayment schedules. Negotiating with creditors is frequently a last resort tactic in financial planning, but it can offer substantial relief to people who are struggling with excessive debt loads and give them a chance to take back control of their financial circumstances.

Accelerated debt reduction can also be achieved by raising income. This tactic entails locating supplementary revenue streams, such as freelance work, part-time jobs, or passive income streams, and allocating the additional funds solely to debt reduction. Individuals may need to look for higher-paying work, take on a side gig, or monetize a skill in order to increase their income.

Increasing sales, cutting operational inefficiencies, or looking for new markets are some ways that firms might increase revenue. The strategy of raising income is very beneficial in financial planning since it enables borrowers to take on debt more aggressively without sacrificing their quality of life or essential business functions. Borrowers can drastically cut down on the time and overall cost of being debt-free by allocating all increased income to debt payments.

Lifestyle adjustment, which entails reducing wasteful spending to free up money for debt payments, is another debt reduction tactic. Since consumer debt is frequently linked to lifestyle expenditures on things like entertainment, dining out, and luxury goods, this strategy is especially pertinent for consumers. A minimalist lifestyle, putting needs before wants, and getting rid of unnecessary purchases are a few examples of lifestyle changes. Reducing non-core expenses and discretionary spending is what lifestyle transformation means for businesses. A mental shift that prioritizes long-term financial security above instant enjoyment is necessary for lifestyle transformation in financial planning. Although altering one's lifestyle can be difficult, doing so is frequently required to reduce debt significantly and avoid taking on more debt in the future.

Another popular tactic that might lower debt repayment expenses is debt refinancing, particularly for mortgages and other long-term debts. Refinancing is the process of switching out an existing loan for a new one with better conditions, including a longer repayment period, a cheaper interest rate, or a different loan structure. A homeowner with a high-interest mortgage, for instance, might refinance to a loan with a lower interest rate, which would cut monthly payments and total interest costs. Refinancing loans is another way for businesses to boost cash flow or capitalize on advantageous market conditions. Refinancing can reduce the cost of debt and make payments easier, making it a useful instrument for debt reduction in financial planning. To ascertain whether the savings outweigh the expenditures, a comprehensive study is necessary, as refinancing frequently entails fees and closing costs.

Another proactive approach to debt management is setting up an emergency fund, which helps avoid taking on more debt in the event of unforeseen needs. By serving as a buffer against unforeseen expenses, an emergency fund enables people or organizations to avoid using credit cards, payday loans, or other high-interest debt. Generally speaking, financial advisors advise putting three to six months' worth of spending away in a readily accessible emergency savings account. When faced with unexpected medical expenses, auto repairs, or a temporary lack of income, people can prevent themselves from getting further into debt by keeping an emergency fund. By stabilizing cash flow during economic downturns or unforeseen disruptions, an emergency reserve can help businesses avoid taking out loans on disadvantageous terms. An emergency fund lowers the risk of future debt accumulation and promotes overall financial health even though it is not a direct debt reduction approach.

Since a higher credit score can result in better loan terms and lower interest rates, improving one's credit score is another crucial component of debt reduction. A number of variables, such as payment history, credit utilization, length of credit history, credit kinds used, and current credit inquiries, are used to calculate credit scores. Borrowers can raise their credit scores over time by concentrating on making on-time payments, minimizing credit utilization, and avoiding submitting too many new credit applications. Borrowers can drastically minimize the cost of debt by qualifying for lower interest rates on future loans or refinance alternatives when their credit score is higher. Credit score development is a continuous process in financial planning that helps reduce debt by making credit more accessible and inexpensive, allowing borrowers to pay off debt without paying exorbitant interest costs.

Public policy can contribute to debt reduction on a social level in addition to individual debt reduction tactics. Regulations that restrict predatory lending practices, like high-interest payday loans, for example, can shield customers from becoming trapped in debt cycles that are impossible to escape. Individuals and families can also benefit from government programs that offer debt relief, financial education, or subsidized loans for necessities like housing and education. Financial stability for firms can be supported by laws that promote access to reasonably priced credit or offer tax breaks for debt repayment. When it comes to financial planning, knowing how public policies affect debt reduction can help people and businesses make wise choices and utilize the resources that are available to them in order to manage their debt.

Accountability and psychological support are also advantageous for debt reduction tactics. Significant stress from debt can have an adverse effect on one's mental health and general well-being. People can maintain their motivation and commitment to their debt reduction goals by having a support network, such as a financial advisor, accountability partner, or support group. Setting attainable goals and acknowledging minor accomplishments along the road is crucial, according to financial advisors. The debt reduction process can appear less daunting and more achievable if big debts are broken down into smaller, more achievable targets. Furthermore, by giving people the information and abilities they need to make wise financial decisions and prevent further debt accumulation, financial education is essential to debt reduction. Reducing debt involves more than just numbers; it also entails altering attitudes and behaviors, which calls for both practical solutions and emotional fortitude.

In summary, there are numerous debt reduction techniques that can be used for various financial circumstances and objectives. Every method offers a unique route to financial stability, ranging from debt consolidation and budgeting to negotiating with creditors and refinancing loans. Although debt reduction calls for commitment, organization, and discipline, the benefits of being debt-free make the work worthwhile. People and companies may take charge of their financial destiny, lessen financial stress, and lay the groundwork for long-term financial success by combining these tactics. In order to assess the most successful debt reduction strategies, make sure that resources are distributed efficiently, and make sure that debt management is in line with larger financial objectives, financial planning and analysis are essential. Individuals, corporations, and governments may all lower debt, enhance their financial well-being, and build a more secure financial future by carefully planning and managing their debt.

Maintaining a Healthy Credit Score

As the foundation for one's own financial stability and development, keeping a high credit score is essential for financial planning and analysis. A person's ability to obtain loans, mortgages, and other financial goods is influenced by their credit score, which is a numerical evaluation of their creditworthiness. A credit score is a quick way for most lenders to determine whether a borrower will be able to pay back their debt on schedule. A high credit score enables people to acquire advantageous interest rates, which lowers the cost of borrowing. A low score, on the other hand, can lead to increased rates or outright credit denial, starting a vicious cycle that could impede financial advancement. As a result, knowing and controlling the variables that impact credit ratings is crucial to financial planning since it influences both short-term borrowing costs and long-term financial results.

Numerous factors affect credit scores, and each one adds in a unique way to the final result. Payment history, amounts outstanding, length of credit history, new credit inquiries, and credit kinds used are the main factors. A person's payment history, which is frequently the most important component, shows how reliable they are in making on-time debt payments. Missed or late payments have a detrimental effect on this component, lowering credit scores and raising suspicions among lenders. Another important factor is outstanding debt or the credit utilization ratio, which shows the percentage of credit used compared to available credit. The credit score can be lowered by high credit use rates, which can be an indication of financial instability and excessive reliance on credit. Furthermore, the length of credit history highlights the borrower's credit management expertise, giving preference to those with a longer, more carefully maintained credit history. The elements are completed by new credit applications and a variety of credit kinds, including installment loans and revolving credit cards. A high number of recent inquiries may indicate financial trouble, which would lower the score.

Financial counselors emphasize how crucial it is to follow best practices for credit use in order to build and preserve a positive credit history. Being on time with payments is one of the simplest tactics. People can avoid missing deadlines by setting up automatic payments or reminders, which is particularly advantageous for those who are in charge of several accounts. Another good strategy is to keep balances low in relation to credit limitations because credit scores are positively impacted by decreased credit utilization. Although aiming for even lower utilization can produce better advantages, financial counselors typically advise maintaining utilization below 30% of the loan limit. Additionally, avoiding pointless queries that could momentarily impact scores can be achieved by exercising caution while starting new credit accounts. Younger people may need to exercise caution in this area by keeping older accounts active, even if they are not regularly used, although early credit establishment and long-standing accounts can also support the length of credit history.

Since credit reports serve as the foundation for credit ratings, managing credit effectively also requires an awareness of how they operate. Examining one's credit report on a regular basis can help identify mistakes that could lower one's credit score if they are not fixed, such as false account statuses or unauthorized accounts. Every year, people are entitled to one free report from each of the three main credit bureaus—Experian, Equifax, and TransUnion—which enables them to monitor their credit profiles without incurring further fees. Accuracy correction is crucial since even minor errors can have a big impact on credit scores. People can dispute differences directly with the credit bureaus, who are legally obligated to look into claims and correct verified inaccuracies. In addition to increasing the accuracy of credit scores, being watchful in this way lowers the chance of identity theft, which is becoming a bigger worry in the current digital era.

Maintaining a high credit score requires effective debt management, which calls for a balanced approach to borrowing and repayment. High-interest debt should be prioritized, according to financial advisors, because it is more expensive and can quickly spiral out of control if not handled promptly. Paying off credit card debt first is advised since, for instance, credit card debt usually has higher interest rates than installment loans. Over time, debt can also become more affordable and manageable by consolidating debts, either by transferring balances to lower-interest credit cards or by securing a personal loan at a reduced interest rate. Consolidation should be approached carefully, though, because taking on additional credit might temporarily affect your credit score, and moving amounts can occasionally result in fines. People can raise their credit utilization ratio and, in turn, their credit score by methodically controlling and lowering their debt.

Balancing the kinds of credit one uses is another aspect of using credit strategically. People who can effectively manage a variety of credit kinds, such as credit cards, auto loans, mortgages, and personal loans, are viewed positively by lenders. This credit diversification demonstrates sound financial management and flexibility in handling different types of debt. However, as the dangers and expenses frequently exceed the advantages, people should refrain from taking out needless loans purely to diversify their credit profile. Rather than pursuing more lines of credit without a clear need, financial counselors advise concentrating on relevant, useful credit that fits with individual financial goals, like getting a house or financing a car.

Despite being one of the most misinterpreted aspects of credit scoring, credit use is crucial to keeping a high score. This measure, which is computed across all revolving accounts, shows the proportion of current debt to total available credit. Even if payments are regularly paid on time, high utilization can indicate financial distress and worse credit scores. On the other hand, maintaining balances below credit limitations raises the score. Financial advisers advise against maxing out credit cards and paying off amounts as much as possible each month in order to get optimal utilization. It's best to spread debt over several accounts rather than focusing it on one for people who must maintain a balance. Additionally, by raising the available credit without raising the amount owed, asking for a credit limit increase on current accounts can help promote utilization if handled properly.

The cornerstones of credit management are budgeting and financial stability, which offer a proactive means of preserving a high credit score. Forecasting income, expenses, and financial commitments is a necessary part of an effective budget, which enables people to set aside money for on-time debt payments and steer clear of late fines or penalties. A carefully considered budget can assist in identifying areas where money can be saved or eliminated, which can subsequently be used to pay off debt or accumulate emergency funds. When it comes to managing credit, an emergency fund is especially helpful because it acts as a safety net to pay for unforeseen costs like auto repairs or medical bills without turning to high-interest credit choices. People can maintain a low credit use rate and maintain their credit score by minimizing their reliance on credit for unexpected costs.

Reducing the quantity of credit inquiries—the checks that lenders perform when assessing credit applications—is another facet of credit management. Regular applications for new credit can have a negative effect because each rigorous inquiry reduces the credit score a little. Although this effect is transient—usually lasting no more than a year—repeated questions may give lenders the idea that a borrower is having financial troubles or is taking on more than they can handle. People can avoid these queries having a negative effect on their score by spacing out applications and only applying for credit when necessary. On the other hand, soft inquiries—like those made by people verifying their own credit scores or by lenders approving offers before they are made—do not impact the score and are free to be made. A more strategic approach to credit management is made possible by knowing the distinction between hard and soft inquiries.

In order to assist people to maintain and raise their credit ratings, credit counseling, and financial education are essential. Expert credit counseling services include advice on budgeting, debt management, and creditor negotiations. These services, which offer a systematic plan for enhancing financial health, can be especially beneficial for people dealing with severe debt or credit issues. For people in need, a large number of non-profit credit counseling groups offer free or inexpensive assistance. Furthermore, self-education via books, online courses, and financial literacy initiatives enables people to make knowledgeable credit-use decisions. Understanding credit mechanisms helps people avoid common problems like depending on high-interest credit alternatives or missing payments out of ignorance, in addition to promoting better credit management.

Digital solutions, which provide real-time access to credit scores, expenditure insights, and individualized financial guidance, have become indispensable for credit management in today's financial environment. Users can monitor their credit ratings, set spending alerts, and examine credit use with the help of tools offered by numerous financial institutions and third-party apps. People may more easily stay informed about their credit health and make timely modifications when necessary, thanks to these digital solutions that streamline the credit management process. Predictive analysis is another feature of certain platforms that recommends ways to raise the score, such as reducing certain debts or modifying credit utilization. People can improve their capacity to uphold a high credit score and make knowledgeable credit judgments by integrating these tools into their daily financial routines.

Planning for the future is just as important as controlling current debt in order to maintain a high credit score. Significant credit is frequently needed for life milestones like starting a business, going to college, or purchasing a home. People can get ready for these milestones without having to pay unreasonably high borrowing fees by actively managing their credit. In order to keep future financial objectives within reach, long-term financial planning should incorporate techniques for preserving and raising credit scores. Additionally, having a high credit score might give people more financial planning flexibility by enabling them to take advantage of advantageous credit conditions or low-interest loans, which will eventually lower borrowing costs.

The practice of managing credit is continuous and calls for commitment, self-control, and careful planning. In addition to offering short-term financial advantages like reduced interest rates and better loan conditions, a high credit score also helps ensure long-term financial stability. A high credit score is a valuable tool in financial planning that can help achieve a variety of financial objectives, such as retirement savings and property ownership. People are more likely to experience resilience and financial stability if they take the time to learn about credit scoring systems and use excellent practices. Anyone can ensure their financial future and maintain a healthy credit score by making educated decisions, keeping a close eye on their credit, and getting professional help when necessary. By remaining vigilant, one may make sure that their credit score continues to be a beneficial influence that supports rather than impedes financial analysis and planning.

CHAPTER VI

Planning for Retirement

The Importance of Retirement Planning

In order to ensure stability and financial security in one's later years, retirement planning is a crucial component of financial planning and analysis. People's proactive retirement planning becomes increasingly crucial as life expectancy rises and economic situations change. Establishing a financial plan that enables people to sustain their standard of living after they stop receiving a regular salary is the aim of retirement planning. This approach necessitates giving careful thought to a number of variables, such as sources of income, costs, prospective medical requirements, and investment plans that can result in sustained growth. People might prevent the financial burden that might otherwise follow their older years by concentrating on retirement planning early in their careers. Retirement planning involves more than just accumulating money; it also entails developing a thorough financial plan that accounts for possible risks and ensures future financial independence.

The uncertainty surrounding public retirement benefits is one of the main reasons why retirement planning is so important. As their main source of income after retirement, many people rely on pensions or government-provided retirement accounts, such as Social Security in the US. These programs, however, might not be enough to pay for all retirement costs, and they frequently run into sustainability issues as a result of demographic changes and economic pressures. For instance, Social Security and comparable programs may be under pressure due to an aging population and falling birth rates, which could lower the amount of payments available to seniors in the future. Personal retirement planning is, therefore, much more crucial because relying only on these programs may result in financial instability. People can better prepare for a comfortable retirement by adding personal savings and investments to state benefits.

A person might benefit more from compound interest, a potent instrument for accumulating wealth over time, the earlier they start retirement planning. When investment returns are reinvested, compound interest is created, producing further returns on the original principal plus any accrued interest. Long-term, this effect can greatly raise the value of retirement funds, especially for those who begin saving in their 20s or 30s. Over several decades, even modest, regular contributions to retirement funds can increase significantly. Because of the power of compounding, a young professional, for example, can build up a sizable nest egg by the time they reach retirement age by making a small monthly contribution to a retirement account. Thus, two essential retirement planning concepts that can result in increased future financial stability are beginning early and making consistent contributions.

An additional crucial element of retirement planning is investment strategy. The risk and possible return of various investment vehicles, including stocks, bonds, mutual funds, and real estate, vary. Younger investors might take a more aggressive approach to investing, putting a bigger percentage of their portfolio into equities or other high-growth assets because they have more time to recover from market swings. To safeguard their earned money, people can progressively switch to more conservative assets as they get closer to retirement, like bonds or fixed-income products. A balanced strategy that promotes long-term growth and protects retirement savings can be achieved by managing risk and optimizing returns with the use of a diverse portfolio. In this regard, expert financial guidance can also be very helpful, as advisers can assist clients in creating an investment plan that suits their individual objectives, risk tolerance, and time horizon.

In order to calculate the amount of funds required to maintain a decent lifestyle, retirement planning also necessitates projecting future expenses. In addition to the usual costs of housing, food, and transportation, retirees may also have to deal with additional expenses like long-term care requirements and higher healthcare bills. For retirees, health care, in particular, can be a major financial hardship because medical expenses tend to increase with age. Furthermore, if not planned for in advance, the cost of health insurance and out-of-pocket payments may put a strain on retirement resources. A clearer picture of the income needed in retirement can be obtained by precisely estimating these costs, enabling people to make appropriate savings. The significance of thorough spending budgeting is further highlighted by the possibility that retirees will wish to set aside money for travel, leisure, or other interests they were unable to prioritize during their working years.

Retirement planning must take inflation into consideration in addition to projected spending, as inflation gradually lowers the purchasing power of money over time. As prices rise, inflation can reduce the value of fixed-income sources like pensions and some annuities, giving retirees less purchasing power. Retirement plans should, therefore, incorporate inflation-hedging techniques, such as investing in equities or real estate, which have a track record of outperforming inflation. Certain retirement accounts, such as IRAs or 401(k) plans, provide investing choices that let people continue to pursue a growth-oriented approach after they retire. Keeping inflation in mind while making plans will assist in guaranteeing that retirement funds will be adequate to cover future requirements, increasing financial stability in the face of growing living expenses.

Since the tax treatment of retirement resources can affect a financial strategy's overall efficacy, tax planning is also a crucial component of retirement planning. Distinct retirement accounts have distinct tax advantages, such as tax-free withdrawals in Roth IRAs or tax-deferred growth in standard IRAs. Based on their income level, current tax bracket, and expected tax rate in retirement, people can optimize their tax status by selecting the right account kinds. For example, because distributions from a Roth IRA are tax-free, people who anticipate being in a higher tax rate in retirement may find it advantageous to contribute to one. However, traditional IRAs and 401(k) accounts, which permit tax-deductible contributions in the present, may be preferred by people who expect a lower tax rate in retirement. Therefore, by reducing tax obligations both during the accumulation stage and when taking withdrawals in retirement, strategic tax planning can assist in optimizing retirement savings.

Planning for unforeseen life events that could affect financial security is another aspect of an efficient retirement strategy. Because life is unpredictable, even the most well-laid retirement plans can be derailed by unanticipated events like a medical emergency, incapacity, or job loss. People can manage these difficulties without using up their long-term savings by having an emergency fund that is distinct from their retirement funds. Additionally, taking into account insurance choices like long-term care or disability insurance can help guard against monetary setbacks. People can make sure that their retirement objectives are still attainable by making plans for the unexpected, even in the face of obstacles.

Retirement planning is also influenced by social variables, such as lifestyle decisions and family obligations. For instance, people who have dependents might have to set aside funds to assist family members financially or pay for their schooling. In a similar vein, individuals who intend to retire early or lead an active retirement lifestyle that involves regular travel could need a greater savings balance to support their objectives. Family dynamics and lifestyle choices are very personal and can have a big impact on retirement preparation. Financial advisors frequently advise people to consider their retirement goals since knowing them can help determine how much money is needed and how to make investments. People can design a retirement plan that is both practical and satisfying by coordinating financial strategies with their personal goals.

Since estate planning deals with how assets and money are distributed when a person passes away, it is strongly related to retirement planning. An estate plan, which may entail drafting a will, setting up trusts, and naming beneficiaries for retirement funds, is frequently a part of a comprehensive retirement plan. In addition to offering comfort, estate planning guarantees that assets be dispersed in accordance with one's desires and lessens the tax burden on successors. Estate planning can help retirees achieve their philanthropic objectives by enabling them to establish foundations or make charitable contributions that will leave a legacy. People can safeguard their financial legacy, help their loved ones, and contribute to causes that are significant to them by including estate planning in their retirement strategy.

Although it is sometimes disregarded, the psychological component of retirement planning is crucial to getting ready for life after work. Many people struggle to adapt to a lifestyle devoid of a set job schedule, which can result in feelings of purposelessness, loneliness, or boredom. Therefore, retirement planning should take mental and emotional health into account in addition to financial planning. To stay active and socially engaged, retirees may find it helpful to develop a routine, take up hobbies, volunteer, or even work part-time. A comprehensive strategy that tackles both financial and personal fulfillment can result in a more fulfilling retirement experience because while financial security is important, so is the quality of life in retirement.

Technology now plays a crucial role in retirement planning by offering tools and information that make the process easier. People may monitor their savings, forecast their future needs, and make well-informed plan revisions with the help of financial applications and retirement calculators. Furthermore, professional advice is now more affordable thanks to robo-advisors and online platforms that provide portfolio management and investment advice at a cheaper cost than traditional financial advisors. These resources can give people the knowledge and understanding they need to make wise financial decisions, enabling them to participate more actively in their retirement planning. People may stay on course for a comfortable retirement by using technology to improve their financial literacy, set reasonable goals, and track their progress.

Financial education is becoming more and more crucial for successful retirement planning as the economy changes and retirement issues grow more complicated. Making smarter decisions regarding retirement savings can be facilitated by having a solid understanding of financial principles like asset allocation, risk management, and tax planning. People can more easily manage the difficulties of retirement preparation with the help of financial literacy programs, seminars, and online courses that provide insightful information about retirement planning techniques. Financially literate people are better able to make wise investment decisions, adjust to shifting market conditions, and safeguard their retirement savings from possible dangers. Therefore, spending money on financial education is a good undertaking that can increase one's chances of having a safe and enjoyable retirement.

Retirement planning is more important than ever in the current volatile economic climate since it lays the groundwork for both financial security and mental tranquility. It is a continuous process that entails investing, saving, and making plans for a day when people won't have a steady source of income. People must take inflation, taxes, and medical expenses into account. Retirement planning is about creating a financial structure that enables people to enjoy their later years without worrying about money, not just about building wealth. People can attain financial independence, accomplish their retirement objectives, and safeguard their legacy for future generations by giving retirement planning top priority within a larger financial strategy. The rigorous financial preparations made throughout one's working life can promote retirement as a period of freedom and fulfillment through strategic investments, careful planning, and a dedication to long-term financial well-being.

Key Retirement Savings Options

A key element of financial planning and analysis is retirement savings, which give people the tools they need to attain stability and financial security following their working years. It is now more important than ever for people to comprehend and make use of their retirement savings alternatives due to the complexity of the economy, higher life expectancies, and the uncertainty surrounding public retirement benefits. Retirement planning is more than just setting aside money from one's paycheck; it also entails choosing the best savings options based on one's time horizon, risk tolerance, and retirement objectives. People can diversify their savings techniques, reduce risks, and possibly improve long-term growth with the range of retirement savings options currently accessible. Every retirement savings choice has its own advantages and disadvantages, ranging from employer-sponsored plans like 401(k)s and 403(b)s to individual retirement accounts (IRAs) and annuities. A more pleasant and secure retirement is possible by choosing the right combination of these accounts to optimize retirement savings.

The 401(k) plan, an employer-sponsored account that enables workers to contribute a percentage of their pay on a pre-tax or post-tax (Roth) basis, is one of the most well-liked retirement savings alternatives. Traditional 401(k) contributions are tax-deferred, which lowers a person's taxable income now and requires taxes to be paid when the money is withdrawn in retirement. Contributions can increase without the immediate tax burden thanks to this tax-deferral benefit, which could hasten the growth of retirement assets. Furthermore, a lot of companies match a percentage of their workers' contributions, which essentially amounts to free money and greatly increases retirement savings. For instance, if a company matches 50% of contributions up to 6% of an employee's pay, then paying the full 6% can result in an extra 3% from the company, bringing the total contribution up by 50%. One of the most alluring features of 401(k) plans is the matching contribution, which gives employees a clear incentive to join and make contributions to their retirement funds.

A 403(b) plan functions similarly to a 401(k) for people working in the public or nonprofit sectors, but it is designed especially for staff members of government agencies, some tax-exempt organizations, and educational institutions. Employees can make pre-tax contributions to 403(b) plans, which, like 401(k)s, grow tax-deferred until they are withdrawn. The possibility of increased contribution caps for workers with 15 or more years of service is one special benefit of 403(b) plans.

Often known as the "15-year rule," this provision enables qualified workers to make extra contributions over the regular yearly caps, offering a helpful choice for people who might have begun saving later in their careers. Furthermore, 403(b) plans typically provide mutual fund or annuity-focused investment alternatives, which can give a variety of options for varying risk tolerance levels and investment objectives. The tax benefits and possibility of additional contributions make 403(b) plans an excellent retirement savings tool for workers in qualified industries, even though employer matches are less common in these plans than in 401(k)s.

Another significant retirement savings option is an Individual Retirement Account (IRA), which is accessible to anybody with earned income, irrespective of sector or employer. While Roth IRAs provide tax-free growth with contributions made on an after-tax basis, traditional IRAs, like 401(k) plans, permit tax-deferred growth on contributions. The tax treatment is the main distinction between these two kinds of IRAs. Depending on the person's income and involvement in other employer-sponsored plans, contributions to a Traditional IRA may be tax deductible in the year they are made. However, required minimum distributions (RMDs) start at age 72, and taxes must be paid at the time of withdrawal. For those who anticipate being in a higher tax band in retirement, the Roth IRA offers a substantial tax advantage because, while contributions are not tax deductible, eligible withdrawals are tax-free. Furthermore, there are no required withdrawals from a Roth IRA, so people can keep their money growing tax-free for as long as they like. IRAs are appealing choices for people who wish to augment employer-sponsored plans or who do not have access to such plans via their employer because of their flexibility and tax advantages.

A Backdoor Roth IRA provides a legitimate way for high-income people or those who want to contribute more than the annual IRA and 401(k) restrictions to finance a Roth IRA even if their income is higher than the eligibility requirements. High-income workers can benefit from the tax-free growth provided by Roth accounts by using this technique, which entails making contributions to a Traditional IRA and then transferring that money to a Roth IRA. The long-term advantages of tax-free withdrawals in retirement may exceed the initial tax expense, even though the conversion process entails paying taxes on the converted amount. For people who value the option to leave tax-free assets to heirs or who expect to be in a high tax band in retirement, the Backdoor Roth IRA is a well-liked method for optimizing retirement savings.

Simplified Employee Pension (SEP) IRAs and Savings Incentive Match Plan for Employees (SIMPLE) IRAs are two more retirement savings alternatives available to self-employed people and small business owners. With contribution limits that are typically higher than those of standard IRAs, self-employed people and small business owners can contribute a portion of their income—up to 25% of compensation—to a retirement account through a SEP IRA. SEP IRAs are a popular choice for independent contractors looking for a simple retirement plan with high contribution caps since they are simple to set up and manage. Conversely, SIMPLE IRAs, which permit both employer and employee contributions, are intended especially for small companies with 100 or fewer workers. Employers must either give a fixed contribution regardless of employee involvement or match employee contributions up to a predetermined percentage. SIMPLE IRAs give small businesses a retirement savings option that promotes employee participation while staying reasonably inexpensive to operate, striking a balance between affordability and structure.

Because of its special triple tax benefit, health savings accounts (HSAs), which are primarily meant for medical bills, can also be a useful retirement savings tool. An HSA allows for tax-deductible contributions, tax-free growth of the funds, and tax-free withdrawals for approved medical costs. By paying for current medical bills out of pocket and letting their contributions grow tax-free, people who make contributions to an HSA while enrolled in a high-deductible health plan (HDHP) can use the account as a long-term savings vehicle. Although non-medical withdrawals will be subject to income tax, HSA funds can be utilized for any purpose without penalty after the account holder reaches age 65. Given the possibility of rising medical costs in retirement, HSAs' flexibility and tax advantages make them a valuable addition to traditional retirement funds. Because they provide a safety net for medical expenses as well as an extra source of tax-advantaged savings, HSAs are, therefore, a wise choice for retirement planning.

Another alternative for retirement savings that offers a steady income stream is an annuity, which is sometimes thought of as a type of insurance against the possibility of outliving one's assets. Annuities are agreements with insurance companies in which the policyholder pays a lump amount or a series of installments in return for regular retirement income payments. Annuities come in a variety of forms, each with a unique degree of risk and potential return, such as fixed, variable, and indexed annuities. People looking for a steady income may find fixed annuities interesting because they guarantee a payout. Conversely, variable and indexed annuities carry greater risk but have the ability to expand in response to the performance of underlying investments. Annuities might offer comfort by guaranteeing a steady income, but they frequently have costs and might not be as flexible as alternative retirement arrangements. For those without access to a pension who desire a steady income stream to pay for necessities in retirement, annuities can be very helpful.

Understanding the distinct benefits and drawbacks of each savings strategy and matching them with one's retirement objectives is the key to optimizing retirement savings. In this process, expert financial guidance can be quite helpful. Financial planners can assist people in determining the best accounts, maximizing tax efficiency, and managing risk in their portfolios. Planning for retirement is a dynamic process that needs to be modified over time to account for shifting tax rules, market conditions, and individual circumstances. People can stay on course to become financially independent and have a comfortable retirement by routinely assessing and revising their retirement plans.

In the end, retirement funds are about establishing the flexibility to enjoy one's latter years stress-free, not only about building riches. People can create a strong retirement portfolio that supports their preferred lifestyle and guards against unforeseen costs by using available retirement savings alternatives strategically, planning carefully, and adopting a disciplined savings approach. The importance of early, persistent, and well-informed savings efforts is highlighted by the priceless piece of mind that comes from knowing one is financially prepared for retirement. Although achieving a secure retirement is a lengthy process, it can result in a happy and worry-free future if the appropriate resources and techniques are used.

Estimating Retirement Needs

A crucial first step in financial planning and analysis is estimating retirement needs, which helps people safeguard their financial futures and continue living the lifestyles they have always wanted after leaving employment. This method entails figuring out how much money one will require to maintain oneself in their post-retirement years, which can include everything from necessities to more individualized objectives like hobbies, vacations, or leaving a legacy for surviving family members. People are faced with the difficulty of making sure they have enough money to meet not only necessities but also unexpected expenses and medical bills as life expectancy rises and retirement periods lengthen. A thorough grasp of anticipated spending and possible revenue streams, along with consideration of inflation, tax liabilities, and investment returns, are necessary for accurately calculating retirement needs. People can adjust their investing and savings plans to reduce the chance of running out of money if they have a solid retirement projection.

Calculating estimated living expenses is a key step in predicting retirement needs. Housing, food, transportation, healthcare, insurance, taxes, and personal expenses are just a few of the many areas that fall under this umbrella. To maintain a comparable quality of living, retirees should use between 70% and 80% of their pre-retirement income, according to several financial advisers. However, this guideline can vary greatly based on specific situations. While some retirees may spend more if they intend to travel, take up new hobbies, or move to a more expensive area, others may spend less because they lead simpler lives or have reduced transportation expenses. Since each category might change based on lifestyle decisions and health circumstances, a thorough breakdown of costs is necessary to provide a realistic projection. For instance, paying off a mortgage may result in lower housing costs, but as people age, healthcare costs typically increase dramatically, which is a big financial worry for many retirees.

Given that medical expenditures frequently rise significantly in later life, healthcare costs are a crucial consideration when making retirement plans. Premiums, deductibles, out-of-pocket payments, and long-term care requirements must all be taken into consideration when estimating these costs because failing to do so might put a burden on retirement funds. Numerous studies indicate that the typical retired couple may require hundreds of thousands of dollars just to pay for their medical expenses. Medicare, long-term care insurance, and health savings accounts (HSAs) can assist in managing these costs, but they might not be sufficient to meet all requirements. For example, Medicare does not cover certain treatments, like dentistry, vision, or long-term care bills, which may require extra preparation for these out-of-pocket charges. Early inclusion of healthcare costs in the estimation process improves projection accuracy and lowers the possibility of financial strain in retirement. Because they are more likely to experience greater medical costs, those with certain medical illnesses or family histories of disease may also need to modify their healthcare estimates accordingly.

Taking inflation into consideration is a crucial component of calculating retirement needs. The cost of living in retirement will probably be higher than it is now since inflation gradually reduces purchasing power. Even modest inflation can have a big influence on the value of funds over a retirement period that could last 20, 30, or even 40 years. A 3% inflation rate, for example, might not seem like much in a year, but over 30 years, it would essentially cut the purchasing power of current dollars in half. People must, therefore, account for inflation when estimating their retirement income in order to maintain a constant quality of living. Depending on historical patterns, this can be accomplished by raising the projected yearly retirement expenses by a specific inflation rate, usually 2% to 3%. Since healthcare inflation frequently exceeds normal inflation, some financial planners advise adopting a slightly higher rate to account for it. Inflation-adjusted retirement estimates guarantee that people are not unprepared for the growing prices of goods and services they will experience in retirement.

Finding every possible source of income is a crucial part of estimating retirement. This covers personal savings or investments, annuities, pensions, and Social Security benefits. Even though the payments may only partially cover living expenditures, Social Security continues to be a significant source of income for many seniors. People can use their earnings records to predict their Social Security payments. The Social Security Administration calculates future benefits based on an individual's work history and selected retirement age. Delaying benefits past the full retirement age might result in a higher monthly payment, so choosing when to claim Social Security benefits is crucial. Employer pensions, which offer guaranteed income based on years of service and salary history, may also be available to some retirees.

Because they affect the growth of retirement savings, investment returns are still another important consideration in retirement planning. Using a combination of stocks, bonds, and other assets to strike a balance between security and growth is a popular strategy for retirement investment. Bonds give more stability with lesser returns, whereas stocks often offer higher returns but are more volatile. Many people switch to a more cautious asset allocation as retirement draws near in order to lower the chance of suffering significant losses. Estimating how much savings will increase over time can be made easier with an understanding of the projected rate of return on investments, but predictions must be reasonable and take possible market swings into account. Assuming, for example, a diversified portfolio's long-term average return of 5% to 7% may be appropriate, even though returns can differ significantly from year to year. People can project their retirement savings balance and assess if it will be enough to cover their estimated needs by accounting for the expected rate of return.

Using a retirement withdrawal rate to determine how much income may be taken out of savings annually without rapidly depleting the fund is a crucial step in evaluating retirement needs. According to the well-known "4% rule," retirees can take out 4% of their assets each year, adjusted for inflation, to make sure their funds survive for roughly 30 years. For instance, after accounting for inflation in later years, a retiree with $1 million in savings could take out $40,000 in the first year. This rule does have some limitations, though, as its efficacy may be impacted by shifting costs, individual circumstances, and market conditions. A 4% withdrawal rate could not be viable during extended market downturns or in low-interest-rate circumstances. For a higher level of lifespan certainty, some financial advisors recommend a more cautious rate, like 3%. Analyzing various withdrawal rates gives people a baseline for managing their retirement expenditures and helps them figure out how much they need to save.

Getting ready for future long-term care requirements is a sometimes disregarded part of retirement planning. Without careful preparation, long-term care services like assisted living, nursing facility care, or in-home care can become unaffordable. One choice that covers these costs is long-term care insurance. However, these plans can be expensive and have restrictions. People can prepare for one of the biggest and most unpredictable costs they may encounter in their later years by factoring in the possible cost of long-term care when estimating their retirement. To cover these expenses, those without long-term care insurance might need to set aside more money or think about other options, such as a health savings account (HSA). Long-term care planning gives retirees and their families peace of mind by reducing the chance that unanticipated medical costs would deplete retirement funds.

The timing of retirement is also taken into account in a thorough retirement estimate. Because early retirement necessitates lengthier savings and may restrict contributions during prime earning years, it can increase the requirement for a larger retirement fund. Delaying retirement, on the other hand, can result in more savings and possibly higher Social Security payments, which can lessen the need for personal savings. One crucial exercise that aids people in determining if they are on track to reach their objectives is estimating the effect of various retirement ages on financial needs. In order to maintain a steady income stream while transitioning to retirement, many people choose phased retirement, which involves progressively reducing work hours. A flexible approach to retirement planning that takes into account changes in health, job satisfaction, or lifestyle preferences is offered by estimating needs based on several retirement scenarios.

In the end, determining retirement needs is a very personal process that takes consideration of numerous aspects and knowledge of both financial and personal aspects. Retirement calculators and other financial planning tools can assist people in projecting their needs, but expert financial guidance is frequently crucial for developing a thorough and practical plan. A financial planner can shed light on intricate issues that can have a big impact on retirement security, like risk management for investments, tax-efficient withdrawal plans, and healthcare cost planning. Since changes in family circumstances, health, or income might affect retirement goals and requirements, it's therefore critical to update retirement estimates on a regular basis. People can make well-informed decisions that promote their long-term financial well-being and stay on track toward their retirement goals by routinely examining and modifying their estimates.

To sum up, calculating retirement needs is a complex yet crucial component of financial planning that enables people to become financially independent and have a good retirement. People can develop a realistic retirement projection that supports their preferred lifestyle by carefully evaluating expected spending, income sources, tax obligations, inflation, and healthcare costs. People can overcome the uncertainties of retirement and ensure a future free from financial anxiety by practicing disciplined saving and strategic planning. An accurate estimate is the first step towards a financially secure retirement, enabling people to take charge of their financial futures and experience the peace of mind that comes with being well-prepared for the years to come.

CONCLUSION

The goal of "Financial Planning Fundamentals: Analysis and Strategy for Success: Strategies for Achieving Financial Goals" is to give readers the fundamental knowledge and useful tools they need to confidently traverse their financial journeys. This book emphasizes that effective financial planning is an ongoing process of analysis, adaptation, and well-informed decision-making by concentrating on the following key areas: risk protection, debt management, investing, saving, and budgeting.

As readers have discovered, financial planning is a customized road map based on individual objectives and situations rather than a one-size-fits-all strategy. Anyone may take charge of their finances by setting specific, attainable financial goals and implementing situation-specific tactics. Small, steady measures are taken at the start of the journey, such as creating a budget that fits personal priorities, putting a debt-reduction strategy into action, and making deliberate investment and savings decisions.

In order to create the groundwork for both current security and future comfort, this book has also emphasized the significance of preparing for life's uncertainties through asset protection and retirement planning. Building resilience and independence via financial planning helps us face life's obstacles with confidence.

Readers are ready to achieve stability and financial success with these resources. I hope that this book will be a useful tool for reaching financial objectives and building a more promising and secure future.

Thank you for buying and reading/listening to our book. If you found this book useful/helpful please take a few minutes and leave a review on the platform where you purchased our book. Your feedback matters greatly to us.

www.ingramcontent.com/pod-product-compliance
Lightning Source LLC
Chambersburg PA
CBHW081958230125
20711CB00006B/993